Titus, Trump
and the
Triumph *of* Israel

The Power of Faith-Based Diplomacy

Titus, Trump
and the
Triumph *of* Israel

The Power of Faith-Based Diplomacy

JOSH REINSTEIN

JERUSALEM ◆ NEW YORK

Cover Design: Leah Ben Avraham/Noonim Graphics
Typesetting: Optume Technologies

Hard Cover: ISBN 978-965-7023-55-6
Soft Cover: ISBN 978-965-7023-31-0

1 3 5 7 9 8 6 4 2

Gefen Publishing House Ltd.
6 Hatzvi Street
Jerusalem 9438614, Israel
972-2-538-0247
orders@gefenpublishing.com

Gefen Books
c/o 3PL Center, 3003 Woodbridge Ave.
Edison, NJ 08837
516-593-1234
orders@gefenpublishing.com

www.gefenpublishing.com

Printed in Israel

Library of Congress Control Number: 2020910370

I dedicate this book to my loving wife, Rebekah

There are many women of valor, but you have surpassed them all.
(Proverbs 31:29)

רבות בנות עשו חיל, ואת עלית על כולנה
(משלי לא:כט)

Contents

Preface

When I was seven years old, I attended a Jewish day school in Dallas, Texas. One day, in our Torah class, we learned that during the famous Exodus from Egypt, many of the Israelites didn't depart with Moses and the rest of their people. They instead opted to stay in Egypt. Apparently they preferred the familiar life and culture there, even though it was bitter and repressive, to the unknown sojourn in the wilderness.

As a young boy, I couldn't fathom the idea: How, after witnessing ten plagues – wherein everyone was awestruck by God's wonders and miracles – could there be Jews who chose to remain behind, enslaved and disconnected from their people's destiny? That bothered me.

The feeling of shock persisted. Even while watching reenactments of the spectacular events in movies like *The Ten Commandments*, I immediately thought about that group of Jews who never left Egypt. And each year on Passover, while sitting with family and friends to commemorate our ancestors' freedom from slavery, it again bothered me.

When I was thirteen, I flew to Israel for the first time. I couldn't wait to finally set foot in my homeland, the place that Moses had begged God to enter. After arriving at Ben Gurion Airport, we drove up to the hills of Jerusalem and into the city.

One of the first places we visited was Kikar Zion, the main square in downtown Jerusalem. As I stepped off the bus, I was immediately captivated by the scene in front of me.

Thousands of Jews from different cultures and countries – America, France, Russia, Ethiopia – were gathered in one place, ambling through the ancient cobblestone streets, shopping at Judaica stores, snacking at sidewalk cafes while the sounds of sidewalk musicians filled the air. This biblical city, the heart of Israel, had become a bustling, vibrant metropolis. Instantly, it was clear to me that God had led us back to Israel, and the predictions in the Torah were being fulfilled in my lifetime. But instead of being overjoyed, I was saddened – the exact opposite of the feeling I had anticipated when arriving. I couldn't contain my emotions and began to cry.

The reason I was so upset was that I felt that my family, and all the people I knew, were like those Jews who had stayed in Egypt – even after God had performed miracles in front of their eyes. In this case, the Jews in America were unable to partake in this new chapter of history, to witness what God was doing for His people in Israel. As a result, they lived a life detached from this reality, far away from the wonders unfolding in the Golden City of Jerusalem.

In that moment, I realized that if you don't look at the world from a biblical point of view, you may miss the story. From that point on, I made it my life mission to move to Israel, and I worked to get back there until I finally made aliyah in 1999.

In 2004, when I started the Knesset Christian Allies Caucus, I aimed to get more people – not just people who read the Bible – to start looking at Israel through a biblical lens in order to better understand the dynamics in the Middle East. More practically, my objective was to mobilize Christians' growing concern for

Israel by creating a framework for political action. This initiative gained momentum, resulting in a shift from spiritual support into worldwide political support.

While observing this recent change in the diplomatic landscape through interactions on my TV show, *Israel Now News*, and while speaking to various groups across the world, I realized that many issues needed to be clarified. The questions came from all sides. Many Christians didn't understand the Jewish perspective. Some were confused about why many traditional Jews keenly collaborated with Christians on worthwhile projects, while Reform Jews, although proud of their Judaism, seemed to work more readily with Muslims than with evangelical Christians.

From another angle, Jews were observing the increasing wave of Christian kindness and enthusiasm to help Israel but were ignorant about the theological motivations behind it. Why, they wondered, are some churches the biggest supporters while others are virulently anti-Semitic, even divesting from Israel? Also, many Jews who supported Israel were not entirely aware of the powerful connection they felt toward the land. They innately comprehended it, aware that just three generations ago, most of their grandparents were religious and that without their ancestors' allegiance to the Bible and their traditions, Judaism would not have survived. But they still needed to clarify their current relationship to the state within a modern context.

On a broader scale, people were puzzled by certain groups, whose ideology should have resulted in strong advocacy for Israel but who instead tried to condemn it. Why, for example, is much of the liberal media so biased against the most liberal country in the Middle East? Their views on a multitude of policies – from individual rights to gender equality to freedom of speech – seem to align with those of Israel, in contrast to the Arab regimes. Yet instead of seeing Israel as a model to promote freethinking and tolerance, that portion of the media relentlessly and irrationally blames Israel for any conflict, while remaining silent about the bloodshed endorsed by its Arab neighbors. Similarly, many university campuses, the centers for Western education and enlightenment, have become breeding grounds for bigotry – filled with angry students picketing, shouting, and protesting this tiny country that thrives amid third world chaos.

Another issue at the forefront of the confusion was the new wave of Christian concern for Israel, resulting in political support. How did this all come about? Most outside observers see only the results but miss what drives the actions. For example, many people know about anti-BDS (boycott, divestment, and sanctions) legislation but don't understand where it came from. And if such a large percentage of the Jews in America are liberal and don't support President Donald Trump, why then is he so supportive of Israel?

President Trump's recent decision to move the United States embassy to Jerusalem really threw people off. Since the time of its conception in Congress's 1995 Jerusalem Embassy Act, the embassy move has been endorsed by Jewish organizations. But for more than two decades, it had been delayed by Republicans and Democrats alike. And when Trump decided to make the move, the ceremony in Israel was attended by seven hundred Christian leaders but only a handful of Jewish leaders. *How did this become a Christian issue?* people began asking me. Where were the heads of the major Jewish organizations?

But to me, being right in the middle of it all for years, the answers were clear. And it was apparent that their confusion could be resolved, once it was filtered through a biblical lens. I then realized the need to put it all together in a book, to connect the dots and clarify and answer some of these questions.

I am often reminded of the memorable scene in *Raiders of the Lost Ark* about the headpiece to the Staff of Ra, a bronze medallion created to reveal the precise site where the Ark of the Covenant was hidden. Without the perfect-size staff and complete headpiece, nobody could determine where exactly to dig. But once the headpiece was placed on the top of the staff in the map room, the sunlight shone through the headpiece and revealed the location. This analogy is one of many for perspective on Israel when it seems impossible for human beings, no matter how intelligent or in what position of power, to make sense of the Middle East.

The fact of the Jewish people coming back to live in Israel after thousands of years in exile is based on something far more meaningful than any Partition Plan, any arbitrary division of land, or any political decision that granted Jewish survivors of World War II a place of refuge. It is essentially tied to the Bible. And without this perspective, people inevitably miss the entire story and make terrible mistakes politically.

A plethora of books and articles about Israel approach the issues from either a political or a religious perspective. But few combine the two perspectives and look at the recent political events through a biblical lens. This book attempts to merge these two viewpoints by exploring the story of the Jewish people, from the time that the Roman emperor Titus destroyed Jerusalem until today, when President Trump recognized Jerusalem as Israel's capital. It illustrates how if you just look at the situation from a different angle, all the previously misunderstood issues become clear, as does the path forward.

PART 1
THE ALLIANCE

CHAPTER 1

Biblical versus Political

Israel is the most misunderstood place on the planet. This tiny ragged strip of land in the Middle East, which not too long ago was mainly desert, provokes a disproportionate amount of curiosity and critical scrutiny from around the world. Politicians in different countries constantly field questions about their stance on Israel and how to solve this country's internal problems, even though conflicts relating to Israel are remarkably small in comparison to the chaos and barbarism within the neighboring countries. Is the peculiar focus on this corner of the world because of Israel's extraordinary success in such a short time? Is it this success that leads to so much resentment and animosity? Or is there such keen interest because this area, while geographically minuscule, is spiritually immense?

Time and again, people from across the globe adopt definitive positions about what's best for Israel and how to move the peace process forward – yet these ideas never work. Then, they sit back and wonder why. *There must be a solution*, they complain. Much of this speculation is simply ivory tower hubris. Trying to solve the problems of some distant state – surrounded by enemies who threaten it with annihilation – from the comfort of your own home, while never needing to lift a finger or face the consequences of such propositions, is absurd enough. But the main reason people cannot understand is that they view Israel as just another country instead of looking at it from a biblical point of view.

Jews are an ancient people. They have witnessed many nations rise and fall throughout history. Yet their faith, traditions, and language remain strong. The story of Jewish survival and prosperity is that of a nation that once strayed from its prescribed path, and suffered unimaginable consequences, yet has managed to stay loyal to God and therefore connected to its roots and its destiny.

Jewish history, as told in the Bible, begins with one couple in Mesopotamia, Abraham and Sarah, whose lives served as a model for their descendants over the centuries. As the prophet Isaiah advised his people, "Look unto Abraham your father, and unto Sarah who bore you, for when he was but one I called him, and I blessed him, and made him many" (Isaiah 51:2).

To truly appreciate the global Jewish experience through the ages, it is essential to first examine and understand the lives of their forebears as told in the biblical narrative. The struggles and journeys of the Jewish people repeat themselves.

Abraham and Sarah stood alone in a world of idolatry, corruption, and violent anarchy. They were persecuted for their beliefs, traveled to Egypt because of famine, and wandered nearly their entire lives. In the very first biblical encounter with Abraham, God commands him to go from "your country, your birthplace and from your father's home to the land that I will show you" (Genesis 12:1). The Bible later refers to that unspecified land as Canaan, which is modern-day Israel. The continuation of the divine declaration to Abraham contains the message that "I will bless those who bless you, and those who curse you will I curse" (Genesis 12:3).

These same struggles, journeys, and principles recur with Abraham and Sarah's descendants, the Jewish people. Through the generations, the core of Jewish existence has been the values that these descendants established: the belief in monotheism – one Creator who serves as the universal God for all beings – and a moral code that places value on human life in this world. Echoing G-d's message to Abraham, blessings have come to those who have blessed the Jewish people, and those people who have cursed them have suffered a bitter end. And like their biblical forebears, the Jewish nation has, throughout the ages, been persecuted and forced to wander from foreign land to foreign land.

This state of displacement from their homeland and dispersal among foreign nations is known in Hebrew as *galut*, or exile. The first notable descent from their native land began when the children of Israel – like Abraham and Sarah before them – traveled to Egypt in search of food. These families settled in the land of Goshen but just a few generations later were enslaved and endured a brutal exile that lasted 210 years. Through a miraculous escape, they were led to their promised land in Israel, only to be displaced again and again. The peak of tragedy occurred when the Roman Empire conquered Jerusalem, destroyed the Second Temple, and sent the Jewish nation into an exile that has continued through the modern era.

The First Temple

The Holy Temple (Beit Hamikdash), prepared by King David and built by King Solomon, was situated on Jerusalem's Temple Mount. For the next 410 years, this building served as the center of spiritual life as well as a Jewish cultural and intellectual center. For the nation of Israel, the Temple was more than a place of worship and gathering. It signified that the Divine Presence dwelled in our midst, the point where heaven and earth met – a permanent fulfillment of the biblical instruction "Build for Me a sanctuary and I will dwell among them" (Exodus 25:8).

Before the destruction of the First Temple in 423 BCE, the prophet Jeremiah had famously declared, "For thus saith the Lord: After seventy years are accomplished for Babylon, I will remember you, and perform My good word toward you, in causing you to return to this place" (Jeremiah 29:10). And that is exactly what happened.

A little more than fifty years after the destruction of the First Temple, the Persian Empire defeated the Babylonians. The Persian king Cyrus the Great then authorized the Jews to rebuild the Temple, which finally began in 353 BCE – seventy years after the destruction of the First Temple. Judea once again became a vibrant and secure Jewish community. The Second Holy Temple stood in Jerusalem for 420 years (349 BCE to 70 CE). Its destruction was the most devastating blow to Jewish sovereignty in Israel.

The Roman Empire was then the world power, with a booming culture and economy. Its remarkable builders and skillful civil engineers produced unparalleled technological and architectural advances. The empire also had a superior military. The Romans attributed their success and dominance to maintaining a good relationship with their gods. As their power increased, they gradually became oppressive toward the Jewish people in the land of Israel. They insisted on instituting paganism, forced consumption of unclean foods, and imposed their cultural practices, many of which were utterly contrary to Judaism.

Within the Jewish community, there were different views regarding how to respond to Roman tyranny; internal strife ensued. The rabbis objected to mounting a rebellion, foreseeing enormous casualties and an unwinnable battle against a massive and mighty army. They pleaded with the other factions to be patient and suffer through the bitter times of Roman decrees. The Zealots, however, believed that it was better to fight and die as Jews than to live under Roman rule.

Beginning in the year 66, those Jews fought fiercely – and they initially found success. Jewish uprisings against oppression became a thorn in the side of the Roman Empire. Eventually, Emperor Nero sent elite legions with the latest weaponry, led by his most distinguished general, Vespasian, along with his son Titus into Israel to crush the revolt. With a force of 60,000 soldiers, the Romans prepared to conquer the country, steadily moving down from the Galilee in the north toward the capital city of Jerusalem. The massacres were gruesome.

In 69 CE, Vespasian seized Jerusalem. After Vespasian became emperor and returned to Rome, his son Titus took command of the troops. The Roman reign over Israel that had begun with heavy taxes concluded in mass murder. The streets of Jerusalem flowed with blood as the Jews were slaughtered and their homes plundered. The Holy Temple, the heart of Jewish life and one of the ancient marvels of the world, was set ablaze and razed. So began the final exile for the Jews, a long journey of almost two thousand years of subservience to foreign nations. But it also marked the miracle of Jewish endurance and prosperity amid the most hostile environments.

This victory over the Jewish people in Jerusalem was especially significant for the Romans, even though Israel was a tiny country and the Jewish people were relatively few. If it had been any other nation, this conquest might not have been so fulfilling for Rome. But conquering Jerusalem represented more than a military success – it was a triumph of a polytheistic civilization over monotheism.

Indeed, through detailed reports of significant events preserved and transmitted through the generations, Jewish tradition describes how when General Titus slashed the curtain of the Holy Temple, he declared: "Where is *Israel's* God?" The Roman leaders likewise touted the defeat of the Jews in Jerusalem as a victory over the God of Israel. In 81 CE, the Romans sought to capture this viewpoint in stone with the construction of the famous Arch of Titus on the Via Sacra, the main street of ancient Rome.

The building project was commissioned by the emperor Domitian, who wanted to memorialize the military victory of his father, Vespasian, and his late brother Titus over the Jews. The composition was also intended to convey the divinity of Titus. Four years later, the arch was dedicated with great festivities. The extravagant monument, serving as a banner to the world of Roman might, was one of the finest artistic expressions of its time. Its design inspired many future triumphal arches, including the famous Arc de Triomphe de l'Étoile in Paris, France.

The two inner panels, made from magnificent Pentelic marble, depict key scenes in the victory over the Jews. One panel portrays the victory parade after the fall of Jerusalem, as soldiers transport spoils from the Temple: a golden menorah along with silver trumpets and other sacred vessels used in the Temple service, such as the fire pans for removing the ashes from the altar and the Table of Showbread. Jewish captives in chains are being marched out of the land of Israel. The opposite panel reveals Titus in a triumphal four-horse chariot led by the goddess of victory

(Victoria) and followed by the Roman people. The symbolic message of success, centered around the Jewish defeat, is clear.

The Roman Perspective versus the Prophecy Perspective

The reason the Romans took such a bold stance and publicized the ruin of Jerusalem is that they were looking only through a political lens. In their eyes, they had squelched the Jewish rebellion, destroyed the religious epicenter of the Jewish people, and expelled them from their land. This, they figured, would be the end of Jewish heritage, culture, religion, language, and autonomy. As with so many other nations before (and after) the Romans, it may have appeared that the Jewish people would fade away and vanish from the Earth. And from a political perspective, this view made perfect sense.

But anyone familiar with the verses and the prophets in the Bible understood that this defeat, along with the resulting exile, was not the end of the Jewish people; it was all part of the biblical prophecy. Though the Jews had been expelled from Israel and would be dispersed among different countries, they would one day return to their homeland. For the Jewish people, the destruction of the Temple and exile from Jerusalem was an overwhelming heartbreak – but it wasn't a surprise. Biblical passages had already cautioned of this time.

The prophets had warned: "Therefore shall Zion for your sake be plowed as a field, and Jerusalem shall become heaps, and the Temple Mount as the high places of a forest" (Micah 3:12). Even in the first generation after the Exodus, Moses forewarns the new Jewish nation that their descendants will one day turn their backs on God and suffer a horrible punishment. "And the anger of the

Lord will be kindled against you, and He will shut the heaven, and there will be no rain, and the ground will not give its produce; and you will perish quickly from the good land which the Lord gives you" (Deuteronomy 11:17).

Yet along with this admonishment came statements of reassurance that no matter what happened, God would fulfill his covenant with them and return them to their land:

> Then the Lord your God will return you from captivity, and have compassion upon you, and will return and gather you from all the peoples, where the Lord your God has scattered you. If any of your dispersed are in the ends of the heavens, from there will the Lord your God gather you, and from there will He take you. (Deuteronomy 30:3–4)

Aware of these and the many other prophecies, Jewish leaders viewed the destruction of the Temple, which impelled the first exile, as the beginning of the dramatic fall that would eventually lead their people to an even greater height. For the Roman leaders, however, it looked like the end of the Jewish story – a confirmation of Rome's resounding dominance over a brash nation that had dared to defy them.

This misdiagnosis of the conflict occurred because the Romans weren't looking at the event in a biblical context. And why should they have? Titus didn't believe in the Hebrew Bible. And because he had no idea what the Bible said – or if he did, did not accept it – he thought he had shown the world that monotheism was false, that the God of Israel was not real, and that paganism and the ideas that Rome embraced had prevailed. This theme of looking at the Jewish people as just another nation rather than through the lens of the Bible recurs throughout history. As a result, the events that happen to Jewish people are often misinterpreted.

In our time, this error shows up concerning the conflict in the Middle East. Since the return of the Jewish exiles to the land of Israel, people tend to view the ongoing unrest in the region *only* as a political struggle. And because it is viewed as such and not as part of the larger biblical narrative, many of the solutions offered do not help to resolve the situation. In fact, they only cause more agitation.

In recent years, for example, a popular solution to the conflict has been the formula "land for peace." The proposition of exchanging land in Israel for the *possibility* of peace, wherein the government gives away land to another nation in the hopes of being left alone, is unheard of in the chronicles of history. People assume that if the intent behind the proposed solution is positive, the outcome will be positive. But any social scientist understands that this is often not the case. In this situation, even if somebody cares deeply about human rights and Israel – which is often questionable – many pitfalls arise from the fact that the politicians suggesting resolutions do not understand the culture in the Middle East or the agenda of the countries with which Israel must contend.

What do the Arabs really want? The Arab media and the Palestinian leadership (whether the Palestinian Authority or Hamas) make clear their intentions to wipe out Israel. They proudly maintain a "pay for slay" policy – offering stipends and benefits to the families of terrorists. Any Palestinian state with autonomy would surely arm itself to a greater degree and continue with its call for the destruction of Israel. The United Nations would defend its right to do so – and Arab nations such as Iran would send arms.

Furthermore, anyone familiar with Islam and the prevailing culture knows that "peace" in that part of the world means something completely different to Arab leaders – that is, a temporary ceasefire until you can attack – whereas to Israelis and Americans, "peace" means coexistence in harmony and long-term sustainability. History has repeatedly demonstrated that whenever Israel transferred land to its enemies, it never led to any peaceful resolution. Rather, every sacrifice of territory was unilateral on the part of Israel and only encouraged its enemies to pursue more violence and try to gain more land. The tally of deaths stemming from terrorism increased. Arab leaders still called for a holy war and advertised their desire to wipe out Israel.

In the end, giving away land in the *hope* of a more peaceful existence amounted to Israel giving up strategic positions, places vital for security, in exchange for a meaningless piece of paper that holds no value in the Middle East, where Islamic culture dominates. The Palestinians have broken every agreement they made with Israel, and Arab nations have a poor record of honoring agreements amongst themselves. Nevertheless, world powers continue to pressure Israel, pushing the flawed land-for-peace initiative, at the expense of human lives.

The Preservation of Life

The immeasurable value of human life is at the core of Jewish ethics. The protection of human life has also been accepted as a fundamental reason for the existence of governments. As the US constitution proclaims, the very first purpose of a government is to secure "the right to life" for its citizens. If we apply this concept to the present conflict in Israel, there is no immediate sign of peace although decades have passed, and despite efforts by world powers to find solutions. In fifty-two years of negotiations, the Palestinians have done nothing to create a political movement that demonstrates they wouldn't be a threat to Israel's security. Western politicians pushing their foreign policies live far away from the tragedies. For them, deaths in the Middle East are merely statistics.

But for the citizens of Israel, their physical existence is at stake. They face the threat of terrorism every second, making every concession a security risk. If, for example, an Arab leader would agree to a new peace treaty with Israel, history has demonstrated that the Arab regimes are unstable dictatorships inclined to uprisings and unpredictable shifts in attitude. Even current allies, such as the leadership in Jordan, can change in an instant. To make real progress toward true peace, someone must first be able to identify the best course of action to most effectively protect the citizens of Israel.

Like any government, Israel has a responsibility to ensure that its citizens feel secure and that their lives will not be constantly endangered. Giving land away exposes all the inhabitants of Israel to more attacks. And when questions of life and death are involved, it is only common sense that one should not take risks for the appearance of diplomatic success, based on what *may or may not* happen later. Therefore, without a reasonable guarantee of future safety, Israel cannot afford to endanger its citizens' safety.

The above reasoning is independent of the Jewish people's love for the land, their legal right to be there, and the fact that Jewish people are biblically and historically connected to Israel. It is a life-threatening issue in which the lives of millions are at stake.

Legal and Political Claims to the Land

In addition to the logical issue of security, there is a strong legal basis for Jewish sovereignty in Israel. This foundation in international law is often unknown, ignored, or left out in the face of a false narrative that is being presented to the world. As the enemies of Israel make incredible efforts to wage a propaganda war and distort the history of the country, the average person becomes less informed about the historical basis for Jews living in the land.

At the core of much of the Arab political rhetoric is the assertion *The land of Israel is ours. We had been living there for centuries until you took it from us.* This story has been accepted by many in the media and pushed in many anti-Israel forums. In the second part of this book, we'll examine the legitimacy of ancestral connection to the land. But first, let's look at some of the significant events underlying the establishment of the modern state of Israel from a legal standpoint.[1]

In November 1917, the government of Great Britain issued the Balfour Declaration, a public statement written by Lord Balfour, the prime minister of the United Kingdom, to support the reestablishment of a Jewish national home in the land of Israel. This declaration was accepted by every allied and associated country at that time.

The eventual pronouncement of Israel's independence as the modern Jewish state was a binding instrument of international law enacted in the San Remo Resolution on April 25, 1920, when representatives of the great powers who triumphed in World War I – France, Italy, and Japan, along with Great Britain – met in the Italian town of San Remo to divide the Middle Eastern regions. This resolution served as the foremost document for Jewish rights and the land of Israel. It was adopted by the League of Nations and signed by fifty-one countries, granting exclusive legal and political rights in the land of Israel to the Jews. Arabs were granted rights to the rest of the Middle East, which amounted to a drastically larger portion.

That binding act of international law was further recognized and incorporated in multiple instruments of international law, namely Article 22 of the Covenant of the League of Nations, the Mandate for Palestine, and the 1920 Franco-British Boundary Agreement.

The principles of international law dictate that once a certain situation has been accepted and the matter is executed, it cannot be readily changed. In this case, the San Remo Resolution supersedes any later UN resolutions. And none of the national and political rights recognized as inhering in the Jewish people have ever been revoked, nullified, or superseded by a subsequent legally valid and binding document of international law.

Later, Article 80 of the United Nations charter recognized the continued unbreakable validity of the rights granted to states or peoples that already existed under international instruments, including the binding act of international law enacted in the San Remo Resolution. As such, all resolutions and agreements violating those rights that have been subsequently adopted by the General Assembly and Security Council are neither legally valid nor binding.

The San Remo Resolution and League of Nations Mandate, along with other supporting subsequent acts, instruments, and agreements of binding international law, legally established the final declaration of the modern State of Israel's independence as the Jewish national home in the land of Israel. This included the Jewish ancestral regions of Judea, Samaria, and Jerusalem. On May 14, 1948, the State of Israel declared its independence and self-governance, thereby exercising its legal right to reestablish the Jewish national home as an independent state in the land of Israel.

Territories legally designated for the Jewish national home under international law, which were belligerently conquered by

Jordan and Egypt in the war following Israel's declaration of independence, *never belonged* to Jordan or Egypt under international law, nor were they ever under their recognized sovereignty.

Contrary to the common misrepresentation upon the end of hostilities in the Six-Day War of June 1967, the Fourth Geneva Convention of 1949, in reference to the laws of belligerent occupation, did not apply to *any area* that formed part of the Jewish national home that Israel had just liberated, in particular the areas of Judea, Samaria, Gaza, and Jerusalem. It is, therefore, legally wrong to characterize the State of Israel as an "occupier" or to suggest that the approximately 750,000 Jews currently living in these areas (500,000 in Judea and Samaria, and 250,000 in what is called East Jerusalem) do so illegally or illegitimately.

The State of Israel appropriately exercised its legal right to declare the city of Jerusalem to be the eternal and indivisible capital of the Jewish national home, thereby ensuring the protection of religious freedom for worshippers of all faiths under Israeli sovereignty.

The legal and political rights of the Jewish people to the land of Israel are abundantly clear. But however substantial these rights may be, they pale in comparison to the biblical rights of the Jewish people to the land. The strongest connection to Israel is not based on any government initiatives, international laws, or resolutions but stems from God's repeated promises to the Jewish people concerning the land of Israel.

From a political perspective, if you have two sides fighting, giving a piece of the land to one party and another section to the other party sounds like a logical solution; in theory, then everyone will be satisfied. But, in addition to compromising the security of Israel, that solution doesn't make sense from a biblical perspective: the land of Israel is the Jewish inheritance, part of a covenant, and we cannot give that away. It is only by changing the paradigm – looking through a biblical lens, not a political one – that we can hope to achieve lasting peace in the region.

An Everlasting Covenant

The first command to Abraham in the book of Genesis entails a journey, away from his birthplace and his father's home, "to the land that I will show you" (Genesis 12:1). Later, a covenant is established.

> As for Me, behold, My covenant is with you, and you shall be the father of a multitude of nations.... And I will establish My covenant between Me and you and your seed after you throughout their generations for an *everlasting* covenant, to be a God to you and your seed after you. And I will give you, and your seed after you, the land of your sojournings, all the land of Canaan, for an *everlasting* possession, and I will be their God. (Genesis 17:4, 7–8; emphasis added)

These verses explicitly relate that (a) the covenant with Abraham is tied to the land; (b) this covenant continues to his descendants; and (c) this covenant is everlasting. Pointing to these passages, one may wonder: God calls Abraham "father of a multitude of nations." Many nations today regard Abraham as their forefather. If so, what is the exclusive connection between Abraham, his covenant, and the Jewish people?

To negate any possible confusion, the biblical narrative quickly clarifies the lineage of this covenant:

> And as for Ishmael, I have heard you; behold, I have blessed him, and will make him fruitful, and will multiply him exceedingly; twelve

princes shall he beget, and I will make him a great nation. But My covenant will I establish with Isaac, whom Sarah shall bear to you at this set
time in the next year. (Genesis 17:20–21)

Isaac's son Jacob is later instructed by God to change his name to
Israel. His descendants, who travel to Egypt, are known throughout the Bible as "the children of Israel." Ultimately, the promised
land they enter adopts this same name.

Throughout scripture, God's promise of the people of Israel
inheriting the land of Israel is repeated: "And it will be, when
the Lord your God brings you to the land which He swore to
your fathers, to Abraham, to Isaac, and to Jacob, to give you..."
(Deuteronomy 6:10).

Later in the book of Deuteronomy, Moses reiterates this connection to the land:

But the land, to which you go over to possess it, is a land of hills and val-
leys, and absorbs water as the rain of heaven comes down; a land which
the Lord your God cares for; the eyes of the Lord your God are always
upon it, from the beginning of the year to the end of the year.... So that
your days may be multiplied, and the days of your children, upon the
land which the Lord swore to your fathers to give them, as the days of
the heavens above the earth. (Deuteronomy 11:11–12; 21)

Before he passes away, Moses publicly appoints Joshua to be his
successor. Placing his hands on the head of his disciple, Moses
transfers his spirit to Joshua. Then God commands Joshua to pre-
pare the children of Israel to cross the Jordan River. Joshua's mission was to enter the land, conquer it, and divide the land into
portions for all twelve tribes of Israel. God assures him of success
in this mission, once again mentioning the promise:

No man shall be able to stand before you all the days of your life; as I was with Moses, so I will be with you; I will not fail you, nor forsake you. Be strong and have courage; for you will cause this people to inherit the land which I swore to their fathers to give them. (Joshua 1:5–6)

The connection of the Jewish people to the land is not only found throughout ancient scriptural passages; it also manifests historically: our forefathers and foremothers are buried in the Cave of Machpelah in Hebron. Bethlehem is referred to in the book of Jeremiah as the place where the matriarch Rachel, who is buried at the northern entrance of the city, weeps for her dispersed children and awaits their return. God then comforts her and promises that "there is hope for your future…your children shall return to their own border" (Jeremiah 31:16).

The current names of cities in Israel retained those Hebrew names mentioned in the Bible. The Jews who settled in Israel descend from the people in the Bible. And for fifteen hundred years, the land of Israel was home to the Jewish people. Just recently, in the City of David, archaeologists uncovered what may be the seal of the prophet Isaiah, along with earlier discoveries of seals bearing the names of Jehucal son of Shelemiah and Gedaliah son of Pashhur, the governors specifically mentioned in Jeremiah chapter 38, who petitioned King Zedekiah to condemn Jeremiah to death. So this heritage is not based on some legend; there is archaeological evidence that Isaiah, Jeremiah, and numerous other biblical figures walked the streets of Israel.

Jerusalem, the capital city and center for Jewish life, was the site of the Holy Temple. Jews were commanded to travel to this holy site for Passover, for Sukkot (the Feast of Tabernacles), and for the festival Shavuot (Pentecost). During these holidays, Jerusalem was packed with pilgrims fulfilling the biblical commandments.

Ever since the final exile, the dates when Jerusalem was captured (425 BCE) and those when both Temples were destroyed were established in the Jewish calendar as days of mourning, fasting, and yearning for its rebuilding. And no matter how far away the country of residence has been, throughout the centuries Jews have faced toward Jerusalem during prayer, three times a day.

In this way, throughout the exile, while wandering from country to country, Jerusalem remained alive in the minds and hearts of the Jewish people.

Biblical Israel and Modern Israel

While the Jewish past is preserved in biblical passages, our present encounters, along with our future, are also foretold. This has never been more evident than today in modern Israel, where the Bible is coming alive. Open any newspaper and read about what is happening in Israel and you can better understand the Bible. Those who believe the Bible can see the connection between modern events and ancient verses – how the prophecies are beginning to become reality.

As a result, there is a growing alliance of people around the world, those who study the Bible, who can place what's happening in this context. At the same time, those who deny the Bible's eternal relevance cannot see the big picture. Because they disregard the biblical perspective, they fail to appreciate what's happening to the Jewish people. They watch the events unfold in Israel, but they don't know where it's coming from. They misinterpret the conflict, unable to explain the excessive attention and antagonism toward this tiny country because they are viewing each event only as a political, day-to-day, realpolitik dilemma rather than from the biblical point of view.

By focusing on the biblical right to the land, I do not mean to diminish the need to consider each issue from a security standpoint, or the political and legal basis of Jewish prerogative to the land. It is only to point out that when people *don't* look at it from a biblical point of view, they cannot see the entire picture and where the world is heading.

The Unforeseen Downfall

Returning to our story of the Roman triumph over the Jews, what the Arch of Titus *doesn't* depict is how two years after their conquest of Jerusalem, the Roman legions endured a major struggle at the edge of the Judean Desert, which became the site of one of the most dramatic scenes in Jewish history.

King Herod, a Roman-appointed governor of Israel, had built a line of fortresses around the country to serve as potential places for his escape in case of Jewish revolt. One of those was the desert palace Masada, spectacularly decorated in the latest Roman style with columns, mosaic floors, swimming pools, and elaborate wall paintings. It stood on the top of a mountain overlooking the Dead Sea and contained servants' quarters, dining rooms, luxurious bathhouses, well-stocked storerooms for food, and twelve gigantic cisterns filled with water.

In 66 CE, Masada was taken over by the Jewish rebels who refused to submit to Roman rule. Following the conquest of Jerusalem and the destruction of the Second Temple, more Jews joined the group. They resisted Roman efforts to displace them and used Masada as their base for attacks against the Romans. With the well-preserved food Herod had stored there, as well as the water from the cisterns, they were equipped to last for the foreseeable future.

In 72 CE, the Roman governor Flavius Silva decided to destroy this outpost. The fifteen thousand members of the Roman camp prepared for a long siege against close to a thousand Jewish men, women, and children who resided on the mountain. After the Romans were unable to break through the wall on the east side, they used thousands of tons of rocks and earth to construct a huge assault ramp against the western side. Then they broke the stone wall of the fortress with a battering ram. The Jewish protectors had built another wall that the Romans could not break because it was soft and yielding. The Romans burned down this wall and prepared to enter the next day.

In the morning, the Romans breached the fortress and discovered a shockingly gruesome scene: rather than fall into the hands of the oppressive pagan regime, the Zealots had chosen death. Only two women and five children survived by hiding, which is how the story came to be known to the famous Roman-Jewish historian Flavius Josephus.

News of this devastating confrontation spread and emboldened other nations to resist the occupying Romans by any means necessary. The Roman Empire never fully recovered from the loss at Masada, and that standoff marked the beginning of the downfall of the Roman Empire.

The Bible presents a recurring theme, an important message that God explains to mankind, beginning with His promise to Abraham: "And I will bless those who bless you, and the one who curses you I will curse." These blessings and curses are magnified when the attitude entails the actions of an entire country, and even more so when it's a superpower. Rome went against Israel and, as a result, was cursed.

History has repeatedly shown that the nations who cursed Israel have been cursed. The rulers and governments who tried to destroy or expel the Jews of their country were, in effect, creating their own collapse. It was only a matter of time before they lost the power and prominence they once enjoyed. On the flip side, the nations who bless Israel have been blessed: America stands with Israel and has seen blessings and prosperity because of it.

The upshot: looking at the Jewish return to Israel as solely a political or territorial dispute is a flawed perspective that can lead to significant repercussions. The first step, therefore, in understanding the modern State of Israel is to view the situation through a biblical lens, recognizing how the battle for Israel is, at its core, a spiritual one. The passion of those who support Israel, and of those who resist it, often stems directly from their view of the Bible.

CHAPTER 2

The Roots of Our Faith

Much as Rome was the superpower of the ancient world, the United States has been the most powerful country in our time, influencing international commerce and setting a standard for many economic metrics. But whereas Roman civilization was based on paganism and idolatry, the United States was founded on Judeo-Christian values and adherence to biblical principles. And because of this strong moral foundation rooted in biblical values, the leadership in the United States can recognize how the current events in Israel are directly related to prophecies in the Bible.

For the same reason, there has always been a natural alliance between America and Israel. These common values inspired Israel to become the only democracy in the Middle East and led the US to become its strongest ally. The general sentiment in America today may appear different than in previous generations. Atheism has gained popularity, and biblical ignorance has become more widespread. Scriptural passages once regarded as sacred are often portrayed by educators as outdated and irrelevant. As a result, some Americans are turning away from supporting Israel. But at the time of America's founding and its early history, the importance of the Hebrew Bible was clear and profound. Biblical values and references permeated the culture and daily life of the colonists. In fact, one cannot properly appreciate the movements and political speeches during the struggle for independence *without* knowing the Bible.

The theme of freedom within the Bible comes from the Exodus story. The New England Puritans identified with the struggle of the Israelites, their escape from Egyptian oppression, and their journey toward the promised land. The colonies sought to model their society after ancient Israel, adopting several legal systems based on the principles in the Hebrew Bible. William Bradford, governor of Plymouth Colony, even taught himself Hebrew in order to read scriptural passages in their original language. Many politicians were also Christian scholars who believed that understanding Hebrew would aid in proper interpretation.

This attraction to and familiarity with the Hebrew language continued through the next century. There is speculation that after the Revolutionary War, some Americans proposed that Hebrew become the official language of the new country. Ezra Stiles, a Newport minister, befriended Rabbi Haim Isaac Carigal, a traveling scholar from the Holy Land who helped him improve his Hebrew. As president of Yale College in 1778, Stiles made Hebrew a required course. He even delivered his first commencement address in Hebrew and Aramaic. By then, the Hebrew words *Urim and Thummim* – the phrase used in the book of Exodus relating to the parchment within the breastplate of the high priest – were already on the Yale coat of arms. Harvard and other schools had also been offering Hebrew courses since the 1720s.

This attraction to Hebrew was more than simply an academic pursuit to understand the language of the Bible. Biblical *ethics* were embedded into the thinking of the founding fathers.

Benjamin Franklin, the Renaissance man, was at the head of the thirteen colonies' movement to create a society based on biblical principles during the Revolutionary War period. In August 1776, while serving on the subcommittee for the design of the Great Seal of the United States – which now appears on the back of the $1 bill – Franklin proposed that the dramatic scene of the Israelites crossing the Red Sea be depicted.

In a letter, Franklin described the design he envisioned, which entailed "Moses standing on the shore, and extending his hand over the sea, thereby causing the same to overwhelm Pharaoh who is sitting in an open chariot, a crown on his head and a sword in his hand…" Thomas Jefferson edited Franklin's design and suggested another biblical image: the children of Israel in the wilderness, led by a cloud by day and a pillar of fire by night. Even though these suggestions were never implemented, they reveal a strong connection to biblical narratives.

In his personal life, Ben Franklin's devotion to the Bible led him to virtuous and fruitful relationships with the early Jewish immigrants in America. For example, when the first synagogue in Philadelphia, Mikveh Israel, was expanding, the local Jews appealed to their Christian neighbors for financial aid. Franklin made a generous contribution to the building fund and helped develop what is now the oldest continuous synagogue in America.

As the early colonists had done, the founding generation looked to scripture for insights into human nature. They attempted to pinpoint principles that could be applied as they established this new society. Many regarded the Bible as essential to self-government and liberty. Benjamin Rush, one of the signers of the Declaration of Independence, wrote that the Bible "is the only correct map of the human heart that ever has been published. It contains a faithful representation of all its follies, Vices & Crimes."

John Adams concurred: "The Bible contains the most profound Philosophy, the most perfect Morality, and the most refined Policy, that ever was conceived upon Earth."

With a common guidebook for morality, Christians and Jews also worked together during the American Revolutionary War. At the time, there were relatively few Jews living in the country – around two thousand in a population of more than two million – but there were those who individually contributed greatly to the cause. One such man was Haym Salomon. His story is not well known, but without him, America as we know it might not have come into existence.

Salomon was the son of Jewish refugees who had fled from Portugal to Poland. In 1772, at the age of thirty-two, Salomon moved to Pennsylvania, where he could practice his religion without being persecuted. He started a successful brokerage company, in which many prominent loyalists were his clients. While active in political and economic activities, he maintained his devotion to Jewish values and community life. He helped found Philadelphia's Mikveh Israel synagogue and served as a member of its governing council. He also participated in the country's first Rabbinic Court of Arbitration.

After being thrown into prison by British soldiers for being a spy, Salomon became severely ill and was transferred to a maximum-security prison. Guarding this prison were Hessian soldiers from Germany, hired mercenaries used by England to fight against the colonial armies. These well-trained fighters were notorious for their brutality. Yet Salomon, who spoke fluent German and served as a translator, was able to persuade hundreds of these soldiers to change sides and fight for the Americans. After his release from prison, Salomon continued his activities to advance America's fight for independence.

The war involved a powerful and wealthy British army against thirteen American colonies with limited resources. During the winter of 1780–81, George Washington wanted to march to Yorktown, Virginia, and deliver a crippling attack to the British forces. But his Continental Army was cold and exhausted. The war chest was empty. The new government had no remaining funds for arms, food, and supplies, and no credit available to it. Surrender seemed inevitable.

Washington then sent for Haym Salomon, who arrived and saw the soldiers without shoes or uniforms. He was informed that Washington needed $20,000 to finance the rest of the war – the fate of the nation was on the line. It was a daunting task to raise those funds in a short time. Yet Salomon was able to negotiate $20,000 in loans – from colonists, several European countries, and his personal assets – which enabled Washington to track and capture Cornwallis, thereby ending the war in 1781. The Treaty of Paris was signed two years later.

Weakened from his time in prison, Salomon passed away at age forty-five, leaving behind a wife and four young children. He had given away all his earnings to support the fight for freedom and died bankrupt. The loans he advanced to assist the country exceeded $600,000, which today would be almost $17 million.

Here is a clear example of how it was not only Christians who possessed a powerful conviction that the royal monarchy was unjust and that the revolutionaries would ultimately prevail against a larger and more powerful military. This Jewish immigrant from Poland, Haym Salomon, believed so strongly in the potential of this country that he was willing to invest all his personal funds to advance the War of Independence.

After the war, Salomon maintained his passion and patriotism, confident that the country that had offered his people refuge and freedom would become a model for tolerance. Although Jewish immigrants coming to the New World had initially faced hardships and discrimination in the early colonial period, they were afforded increasingly more rights and opportunities until they eventually enjoyed full equality and protection under the law. Before his death, Salomon led an effort to remove the test oath that prevented Jews from holding public office. Responding to anti-Semitic slander aimed at Jewish patriots, he was quoted in the Philadelphia newspaper: "I am a Jew; it is my own nation; I do not despair that we shall obtain every other privilege that we aspire to enjoy along with our fellow-citizens."

His story reminds us that certain values – such as religious freedom, equality, and individual rights – are more important than wealth. His contribution to America was memorialized with a bronze sculpture in Heald Square, Chicago, depicting General George Washington standing with the two main financiers of the American Revolution: Robert Morris and Haym Salomon. Inscribed on a plaque on the base of the monument are the words "Symbol of American tolerance and unity and of the cooperation of people of all races and creeds in the upbuilding of the United States."

This unity and alliance between different religions, born from a strong biblical connection, continued through the country's development. Perhaps no American president has been fonder of the Jewish people than Abraham Lincoln, who also had a profound respect for and knowledge of the Bible. In his youth, Lincoln had studied the Hebrew scriptures and would often quote from the prophets during his public speeches. According to his wife, Mary Todd Lincoln, in his last conversation just before he was killed,

Lincoln expressed the desire to visit the Holy Land, concluding that "There is no place I so much desire to see as Jerusalem."

In looking at American history, it's clear the themes of the Bible had an influence on the mindset of the founders and leaders. And while the US government has never promoted any specific faith, certain principles were so central to the foundation of the United States that they were engraved on its coins and printed on its currency. The phrase "In God We Trust" still appears on every dollar bill. Today, certain states (among them Texas and Arkansas) have authorized monuments displaying the Ten Commandments on government grounds, another reminder of the values the founding fathers and citizens held dear.

Two Conflicting Prophecies

Looking at the Bible as a guidebook entails not only embracing its moral system but understanding pertinent prophecies. There are two general prophecies in the Tanach (the canon of Hebrew scriptures) that, when placed side by side, seem to be incompatible. The first prophecy speaks of the Jewish people being thrown out of the land of Israel, exiled to the far corners of the Earth, and cursed among the nations as a punishment for turning against God. This is a recurring theme throughout scripture:

> And the Lord will scatter you among the peoples, and you will be left few in number among the nations, where the Lord will lead you away. (Deuteronomy 4:27)

> ...and I scattered them among the nations, and they were dispersed through the countries... (Ezekiel 36:19)

> But I scattered them with a whirlwind among all the nations whom they had not known, and the land was desolate after them, so that nobody passed through nor returned; for they laid the pleasant land desolate. (Zechariah 7:14)

The other type of prophecy, the continuation of the Jewish fate, relates that these same people will be gathered from all over the Earth and brought back to the land of Israel – the same location from where it was exiled – and reunite there, speaking the same language and observing the same religion.

> Therefore, so said the Lord God: Now I will bring back the captivity of Jacob, and have compassion on the whole house of Israel, and I will be jealous for My holy Name.... When I have brought them back from the peoples, and gathered them out of their enemies' lands, and am sanctified in them in the sight of many nations. And they shall know that I am the Lord their God, in that I caused them to go into captivity among the nations, and have gathered them unto their own land; and I will not leave any one of them there; neither will I hide My face any more from them; for I have poured out My spirit upon the house of Israel, says the Lord God. (Ezekiel 39:25, 27–29)

Now, what makes the second prophecy puzzling is that if you take a people and kick them out of their homeland, throw them to the far corners of the Earth, and have them undergo horrible hardships for thousands of years, that is usually the end of the story. Eventually, those people assimilate. They learn to speak a new language, forget their heritage, and lose the ability to distinguish themselves. How much more so, when they are constantly discriminated against, attacked, and murdered.

What are the chances that this same people, two thousand years later, would come back to their original land, speak the same language as their Bible, and remain conscious of their history and loyal to their heritage and religion? The likelihood of a people being torn apart, scattered across the globe, living under the control of foreign governments, then regathering two thousand years later in the original location is a near impossibility.

For these reasons, there were plenty of people who, after witnessing the passing of the first prophecy, doubted the fulfillment of the second. Yet beginning in 1948, that's exactly what happened. The Jewish people returned to Israel from all across the world, after being cursed by the nations, surviving hostile anti-Jewish governments in every generation – from the Mesopotamians to the Babylonian kings, the Roman legions to the Catholic Church in Spain, the Nazis, and the former Soviet Union – that tried to stamp out Judaism.

When people today think of anti-Semitism, the natural and immediate association is with the Holocaust, which is still relatively fresh. And the atrocities of the Nazis against Jews have a unique place in history due to their sheer cold-blooded orchestration, the systematic and widespread collaboration, and long-term sustainment of the horror. For these reasons, memorial museums have been established across the world, and slogans of "never again" remind us of the vigilance required to prevent another vicious attempt to exterminate the Jewish people.

But the waves of horrible atrocities, abuse, and persecution against the Jewish people are not reserved to that most recent monumental catastrophe; there has been a continual pattern of persecution throughout history. As a result, Jews have fled one land, settled in another, thrived there and thought they were safe, then suddenly were expelled or killed.

Among the worst events were the Crusades at the end of the eleventh century. At that time in Europe, there were plenty of unemployed knights, mercenary soldiers trained to kill. The Catholic Church then supported a "crusade," which entailed organizing these soldiers and marching them to the land of Israel to seize it from the Muslims. In 1096, the first Crusade took place. Along the way, these brutal religious warriors murdered Jews, decimating communities in France and Germany as they gashed their way through European towns. When they finally reached the land of Israel and conquered the Holy City, they herded the Jews into a synagogue and set it ablaze.

Spain under Muslim rule marked a peaceful and prosperous period for the Jews who lived there. They were financially successful, held prominent positions within the government, and Jewish life flourished. That all changed when the intensely anti-Semitic Roman Catholic Spaniards took control of the country. In 1391, massacres initiated by the sermons of rogue cleric Ferrand Martinez swept across Spain. Thousands of Jews were murdered, others were forced to convert, and many escaped to Portugal, North Africa, and other lands throughout the Mediterranean Basin.

During the next century in Spain, the Jews were increasingly persecuted, given a choice to convert or to flee the country. After enjoying generations of affluence, many Spanish Jews, reluctant to leave their land and comfortable life, opted to convert. But even then, the Inquisition aimed to root out anyone who might be secretly practicing Judaism. During this process, Jews were tortured and burned publicly. Eventually, an edict was issued that by July 31, 1492, all Jews had to leave the country.

Thus the pattern continued. Jewish life in Spain, where so many families had resided comfortably since the second exile, abruptly ended. Many Spanish Jews, among them great scholars, moved to the land of Israel. They settled in Hebron, Jerusalem, and Safed. The Inquisition and expulsion of Jews from Spain represented one of the greatest tragedies in Jewish history. But it was also a massive loss for Spain. Within a century, Spain became a second-rate country, never to recapture the prestige it had enjoyed while hosting a large Jewish population.

In 1648, a Ukrainian soldier by the name Bohdan Khmelnytsky mounted a revolt against the Polish landlords who controlled the Ukraine. The Polish landlords had hired Jews to run their farms and businesses, which placed these Jews at odds with the Ukrainian and Polish people, who already harbored hatred for the Jews. In his rebellion, Khmelnytsky and his forces slaughtered as many as 250,000 helpless Jews in Eastern Europe and displaced hundreds of thousands of others.

This disaster destroyed Jewish infrastructure in Ukraine, Poland, and Lithuania. Entire communities disappeared. Jews had lived in Eastern Europe for more than four hundred years, and everything seemed wonderful. They had good jobs and autonomy, and the Polish kings had promised to protect them. Suddenly, everything went up in flames with violent attacks – a bitter reminder of their enduring exile.

The 1880s marked a period of revolution in Russia, which brought another wave of anti-Semitism. Under the influence of the Russian Orthodox Church, which was officially anti-Semitic, the Jews endured horrible oppression – decrees, harsh taxes, and their places of residence limited to the Pale of Settlement, which amounted to a large Jewish ghetto in western Russia. Jews were forbidden to have certain professions or attend universities. Along with these discriminatory laws came pogroms.

The term "pogrom" comes from similar Russian words that mean to wreak havoc; devastation; destruction. Historically, the term refers to planned massacres of Jews by local non-Jewish populations that took place in the Russian Empire and in other countries. This violence was often organized by government authorities and encouraged by the police. Jews were killed and raped, their property was looted, and their houses pillaged and burned. The Jews of Eastern Europe saw no way out.

In the late nineteenth century, pogroms swept the Russian Empire, consuming hundreds of thousands of lives. There is hardly a town or village in Europe connected to the Jewish past whose soil is not soaked with Jewish blood and tears. But according to Jewish tradition, disasters will befall the Jewish people before the arrival of the Messiah, much like birth pangs before a beautiful child emerges from the womb. Many saw the Holocaust as the final blow and the return to the land of Israel as the forerunner to a new era.

Regarding this return to the land of Israel – the fulfillment of the second prophecy mentioned above – a common perception is that this influx involved European Jews fleeing after the war. But in fact, Jews moved from all over the world – Russia, Yemen, Iraq, Ethiopia, and Morocco – all with different cultures and characteristics.

The motivation was not only to escape persecution – there were positive reasons, too. Many Jews who arrived from America, for example, were leading good lives, but they decided to make aliyah (a spiritual ascent) because they believed in the prophecy and wanted to take part in its fulfillment. Jews continued to arrive in Israel from America, Canada, Australia, South Africa, England, South America – from all four corners of the Earth, just as the biblical passages had predicted: "And He will raise a banner to the nations, and will assemble the dispersed of Israel, and gather together the scattered ones of Judah from the four corners of the Earth (Isaiah 11:12).

Replacement versus Covenant Theology

One of the questions I'm most frequently asked is why there is such an upsurge of Bible-believing Christians who strongly come out in support of Israel in the world, while many mainstream churches criticize Israel and even promote anti-Semitism. The Presbyterian Church, for example, divests from Israel. There's a Catholic community that has recognized a Palestinian state, and Pope Francis praised Mahmoud Abbas, the terrorist head of the Palestinian Authority, as an "angel of peace." What is the theological division within Christianity that causes some Christians to be so incredibly supportive of Israel and others to be so antagonistic?

To begin, we can divide the modern Christian movements into two general groups: mainline Christians and "Bible-believing Christians." Bible-believing Christians, often called evangelicals, include Baptists, Pentecostals, Charismatics, and some Protestants. The mainline churches include Greek Orthodox, Episcopalian, Anglican, Presbyterian, Catholic, and Russian Orthodox. The theological differences between them, regarding Israel and the Jewish people, stem from how they view the covenant between God and the Jewish people.

The mainline churches acknowledge that there was a covenant between God and the Jewish people. But they believe that once the Jews were kicked out of their land, God broke the covenant and established a *new* covenant with their church. That church then replaced the Jewish people, becoming "the new Israel" and heir to all the blessings that were originally given to the Jews in the Bible. The early church fathers consistently preached this doctrine, pointing to the destruction of the Second Temple – personified in the Arch of Titus – as a sign that God was forever finished with the children of Israel.

The Bible-believing Christian churches reject the position of replacement theology and regard the covenant that God made with the Jews as eternal and the gift of the land as "an everlasting possession," as scripture explicitly describes in Genesis 17:7–8. It is only logical, they point out, that God would not establish a covenant, only to break it. How then does this idea fit into the belief system of Christianity? Bible-believing Christians consider themselves "grafted" into the original covenant with Israel. They didn't replace the Jewish people; they are part of their original covenant, which continues to this day.

For centuries, these two perspectives have been focal points of conflict within the church. As a result, many of the mainline churches are generally anti-Israel, while the evangelical churches are extremely supportive of the Jewish state. This support for Israel has served them well in recent years, helping to advance their theological views.

Mainline branches of Christianity once comprised around 99 percent of all the churches, and the tiny remainder – the Bible-believing Christian churches of evangelicals and Baptists – were often ridiculed for claiming that God maintains the covenant with the Jewish people. When Israel gained its independence, there were around six million evangelical Bible-believing Christians. Today, there are six hundred million.

This rapid revival was sparked in 1948, when the Bible-believing groups proclaimed that, with the establishment of Israel as a Jewish state, God had brought the people of Israel back to their land to reestablish Jewish sovereignty there. These evangelicals then turned to their fellow Christians and, in effect, said: *Look! We were right all along. The new State of Israel is the fulfillment of scriptural prophecies. God has kept the covenant that he swore to Abraham and his descendants – and we are grafted into that covenant.*

Evangelical Christians then began successfully persuading people around the world, mostly other Christians, to adopt their way of thinking by calling attention to the events in the land of Israel – a sign that the Jewish people are truly God's chosen people, as stated in the Bible, and that the promise made in ancient times was being kept. It's therefore necessary, these Bible-believing churches explain, to recognize that the God of Abraham, Isaac, and Jacob is true; that the Hebrew Bible is true; and that the prophecies are coming true.

As a result, millions of people, mostly mainline Christians, began to adjust their perspective. This had a significant effect on the Catholic Church, which softened its stance on Jews. The three most recent popes have even stated that the covenant with the Jewish people is irrevocable. In the last seventy years, the number of evangelicals has radically increased, and they're the fastest-growing religion in the world today.

Examining the two seemingly incompatible prophecies above, some mainline churches thought that once the Jewish people had been kicked out of Israel, it was impossible that they would ever return there to reestablish themselves as a nation. The evangelicals, however, believed it would happen.

The Jewish people certainly believed it was going to happen, as promised in the Torah. Even those passages speaking about the curses make a point to mention that the covenant will never be abrogated:

> But despite all this, when they are in the land of their enemies, I will not reject them, neither will I abhor them, to completely destroy them, and to break My covenant with them; for I am the Lord their God. But for their sake I will remember the covenant with their ancestors, whom I brought out of the land of Egypt in the sight of the nations, to be their God: I am the Lord. (Leviticus 26:44–45)

Therefore, throughout the journey of exile, even during the harshest environments, there was always a faithful remnant of the Jewish people. Indeed, wherever in the world they have resided, observant Jews have prayed three times a day, facing Jerusalem, beseeching God to fulfill His promise and speedily return them to the land of Israel. The siddur, the standard Jewish prayer book, is filled with passages containing this theme: "Return in mercy to Jerusalem Your city... May our eyes behold Your return to Zion..." At the conclusion of every Passover Seder (as well as every Yom Kippur service), Jews utter in unison the famous phrase: "Next year in Jerusalem."

This connection to Jerusalem has been embedded into the Jewish consciousness. Even traditional celebrations are accompanied by some brief remembrance of the Temple's destruction, because without Jerusalem, any joy is incomplete. For this reason, at Jewish weddings, the groom places a glass wrapped in cloth under his foot and smashes it into pieces to remind everyone present that even at the height of personal happiness, we must remember the exile from Jerusalem and yearn to return there. Other Jewish customs instituted to remember the Temple's destruction include leaving a small unfinished square space whenever one builds a home to serve as a visual reminder of exile.

Jews have always held strong to the belief that their mass return to Israel was inevitable. And once it began to happen, many Christians who believed in the words of the Hebrew Bible joined them in recognition that God keeps his covenant.

Christian Zionism

This support for Israel by evangelicals also has historical roots. Many of those involved in the founding of the State of Israel who weren't Jewish were Bible-believing Christians willing to translate their beliefs into political action. We previously mentioned a notable Jew who helped finance America's War of Independence, reflecting the cooperation of Jews and Christians with shared values. A similar alliance surfaced in the creation of the modern State of Israel. While Theodor Herzl is commonly regarded as the founder of modern Zionism, without the assistance of a Christian pastor named William Hechler, this Jewish Zionist might have remained an unknown journalist.

In 1894, as a featured columnist for the most influential liberal newspaper in Austria, the *Neue Freie Presse*, Herzl was assigned to travel to Paris and cover the infamous Dreyfus trial. There, he encountered the citizens of France reverting to primitive anti-Semitism, as mobs shouted, "Death to the Jews." This realization prompted Herzl to further ponder the cause of anti-Semitism and its remedy. His solution to the Jewish problem was to push for an independent Jewish state.

Initially, his ideas were not well received by the Jewish leaders of Europe. To be successful, Herzl knew he would need to publicize his message by connecting to important decision-makers – the European aristocracy, princes, and dignitaries. But he had no idea how to reach them. At one point, he was introduced to Hechler, an English clergyman who was chaplain of the British embassy in Vienna. After reading Herzl's just-published book, *Der Judenstaadt*, in early March 1896, Hechler's response changed the course of history – and of modern Zionism.

Hechler regarded the Zionist movement as a "prophetic crisis." Years earlier, Hechler had predicted that Palestine would be returned to the Jews. After meeting Herzl, he immediately hurried to the British ambassador in Vienna and told him, "the foreordained movement is here!" Herzl's proposal for an independent

Jewish state – a national rebirth in the land of Israel – came as his solution to anti-Semitism. Hechler's involvement was inspired by his faith in the Bible. The two men reached the same conclusion from different angles, but both had a sincere interest in ensuring the welfare of Jews by leading them back to Israel.

The cooperation between these two paved the way for the creation of a Jewish state. Many onlookers at the time couldn't understand how Herzl, an unknown journalist, was getting audiences with leaders in upper society and was able to make friends with influential people. He wasn't an influential figure himself, yet he was busy meeting with the king of Prussia and members of the British establishment. But, behind the scenes, the man setting up meetings for him was Hechler. For this reason, Hechler is often referred to as the founder of modern Christian Zionism.

Later, this sort of political collaboration between Jewish and Christian leaders, driven by biblical ideals, showed up when Chaim Weizmann was able to influence Arthur Balfour to obtain British support for the Balfour Declaration. Such collaboration has gained unprecedented momentum in recent times: Reuven Rivlin, the current president of Israel, announced while serving as the Speaker of the Knesset that since Christianity was born out of Judaism, we share the same roots and accept the same passages in the Hebrew Bible – including those that predicted how the Jewish exiles would return to their land. This common perspective, he explained, creates a natural alliance between these two groups of people.

The cultivating of strong relationships between Jews and Christian Zionists is especially fertile today in the United States, a nation embedded with Judeo-Christian values from the time of its founding. The spirit of unity and faith permeated America's original doctrines, its currency, its expressions of allegiance, and the leaders who embraced Hebrew and longed to visit Jerusalem. Unlike Rome, the United States, due to its rich history, can clearly view the current events in Israel through a biblical lens. From this viewpoint, the cooperation between Jews and Christians has enabled the success of both countries to continue.

CHAPTER 3

Prophecy Fulfilled

When it comes to success, there's surviving and there's thriving. The fulfillment of the first series of biblical prophecies – being displaced from the land of Israel and scattered across the world – entailed a long and bitter journey in exile for thousands of years. Jewish people needed to survive the Babylonians, the Greeks, the Romans, the Spanish Inquisition, the Crusades, and decades of bloodshed throughout Europe and Russia.

Today, the Roman Empire is long gone. So are many other nations that tried to destroy the Jews. And despite the historical tragedies that assaulted the Jewish people, once they finally regathered in Israel – setting the stage for the second set of prophecies – the nation was, once again, ready to thrive.

Entering the land of Israel, a barren terrain, there were many challenges. Now, the remnants of this ancient people who had been gathered from around the world, a mix of cultures, languages, and backgrounds, would need to start from scratch. But, as the ancient prophets had reassured them, the Jews began to build themselves up: "And it shall come to pass that [just] as you were a curse among the nations, O house of Judah and house of

Israel, so will I save you, and you shall be a blessing; fear not, but let your hands be strong" (Zechariah 8:13).

For the past seventy-two years, Jews from across the globe immigrated with their families, whether to escape persecution or simply for the love of the land – setting the stage for the second prophecy.

> And it shall come to pass, when all these things come upon you, the blessing and the curse, which the Lord your God has set before you, and you take them to heart while among all the nations where the Lord your God has driven you, and you shall return to the Lord your God, and hearken to His voice according to all that I command you this day, you and your children, with all your heart and with all your soul; that then the Lord your God will bring back your exiles and have compassion upon you, and will return and gather you from all the nations, where the Lord your God has scattered you.

> Even if your exiles are at the ends of the heavens, from there will the Lord your God gather you, and from there will He fetch you. And the Lord your God will bring you into the land which your fathers possessed, and you will possess it; and He will do good to you, and make you more numerous than your fathers. (Deuteronomy 30:1–5)

Beginning in 1948, the world watched as the Jewish people began to return to their homeland from the far corners of the Earth. They came there from the north and south, the east and west, "on the wings of eagles" – or airplanes, as we see today – just as the ancient prophecies described. Once this second prophecy occurred, a tidal wave of other prophecies found in scripture began to be fulfilled. It is as if the second prophecy – the return of Jews to Israel, the settling of the land, and establishment of Jewish sovereignty there – was needed to effect the next series of prophecies, which are swiftly unfolding before our eyes today.

Survival and Revival

To appreciate the connection between the scriptural predictions and the current events, let's examine some key passages, beginning with a famous scene from the book of Ezekiel. God takes the prophet to a valley that is full of dry bones. Standing there, Ezekiel has a vision, and God miraculously turns the bones into flesh, bringing them to life.

> So said the Lord God to these bones: Behold, I will cause breath to enter you, and you will live [again]. And I will lay sinews upon you, and will bring up flesh upon you, and cover you with skin, and put breath into you, and you shall live; and you shall know that I am the Lord. (Ezekiel 37:5–6)

> So I prophesied as He had commanded me, and the breath came into them, and they lived, and stood on their feet, an exceedingly great host. Then He said to me, "Son of man, these bones are the whole house of Israel; behold, they say, 'Our bones have dried up, our hope is lost, we are clean cut off'." (Ezekiel 37:10–11)

In other words, God is explaining to the prophet that this supernatural demonstration should serve as a message to the nation of Israel suffering in exile, symbolized by the dry bones. Though they may feel that their bones have become dried up from the troubles – hopeless and doomed – God will nevertheless revive them. This revival is the return to their homeland. "Therefore, prophesy and say to them: So says the Lord God: Behold, I will open your graves, and cause you to come up out of your graves, O My people; and I will bring you into the land of Israel" (Ezekiel 37:12).

The shadowy description of dry bones rising recounted in the book of Ezekiel may once have appeared to readers as legend or metaphor. But then, in the aftermath of the Holocaust, in which six million European Jews had been systematically murdered, horrifying photographs and films were discovered, and images of walking skeletons rising from the concentration camps began circulating. Many of these survivors returned to the land of Israel, just as Ezekiel's prophecy described.

Those who returned to Zion, having emerged from a living nightmare, could rejoice in a new beginning. And, as the rest of the world looked on in wonderment, they could detect that God had rescued His people once again from destruction. Today, Bible-believing Christians observe the results of these events unfolding in the land of Israel. They interpret the scriptures and respond by saying, *Look what God is doing in Israel – and how the prophecies are unfolding.* The Jewish people can likewise appreciate these wonders and say, *Wow, look what God has done for us* – echoing the famous lines in Psalms:

> A Song of Ascents. When the Lord brings back the captive ones of Zion, we will be like dreamers. Then our mouths will be filled with laughter and our tongues with singing; then they will say among the nations: "The Lord has done great things with these." (Psalms 126:1–2)

> Hear the word of the Lord, O nations, and declare it in the islands from afar, and say, "He that scattered Israel will gather them and watch over them as a shepherd does his flock. For the Lord has ransomed Jacob and redeemed him from the hand of him that is stronger than he." (Jeremiah 31:9–10)

The initial return to the land, while celebrated, was only the beginning. The next stages involved establishing sovereignty, settling, and developing the country. How those stages have occurred are also linked to several biblical passages and prophecies. There is a verse in the book of Isaiah that hints at this rapid rebirth in Israel: "Who has heard such a thing? Who has seen such things? Is a land born in one day? Is a nation born at once? For as soon as Zion travailed, she brought forth her children" (Isaiah 66:8).

On the morning of May 14, 1948, the Jewish people proclaimed their independence in their land – establishing the first Jewish state in two thousand years. The United States immediately recognized the new state, just twenty-three hours later, creating an instant alliance. The *New York Times* wrote, "In one of the most hopeful periods of their troubled history the Jewish people here gave a sigh of relief and took a new hold on life when they learned that the greatest national power had accepted them into the international fraternity."

So the nation was, in effect, created in one day. We have also seen a rapid and astounding prosperity in what was a barren land just a short time ago.

The Deserts Bloom

For visitors to Israel today, it is hard to imagine what it looked like a century ago. The transformation of the land of Israel in such a short time has been astounding. One of the more mysterious passages in Isaiah 35 can then be appreciated:

> The wilderness and the parched land shall be glad; and the desert shall
> rejoice, and blossom as the rose. It shall blossom abundantly, and rejoice,
> even with joy and singing; the glory of Lebanon shall be given unto it,

the excellency of Carmel and Sharon; they shall see the glory of the Lord, the excellency of our God. (Isaiah 35:1–2)

In previous generations, the paradoxical phrase in this prophecy may have been taken as poetic – a desert, by definition, shouldn't blossom. But one only needs to look at the descriptions of the land of Israel over the past few centuries to realize the modern-day miracles that have taken place.

In 1867, the great American writer Mark Twain traveled with a church group to Europe and the Middle East. While visiting the Holy Land, he recorded his observations, in what later was published as *Innocents Abroad*, which is still among the best-selling travel books of all time. Throughout the book, he describes the ugliness and emptiness of the land:

> [a] desolate country whose soil is rich enough, but is given over wholly to weeds – a silent, mournful expanse…. A desolation is here that not even imagination can grace with the pomp of life and action…. We never saw a human being on the whole route…. There was hardly a tree or a shrub anywhere. Even the olive and the cactus, those fast friends of the worthless soil, had almost deserted the country.

Twain did not refrain from expressing his distasteful impressions of the biblical land of milk and honey. "Of all the lands there are for dismal scenery, I think Palestine must be the prince," he wrote. "Can the cure of the Deity beautify a land? Palestine sits in sackcloth and ashes. Over it broods the spell of a curse that has withered its fields and fettered its energies."

While Twain's descriptions are perhaps the most famous personal accounts in modern history, other travelers over the centuries had recorded similar impressions. Rabbi Moses ben Nachman (better known as Nachmanides) was one of the leading medieval Jewish scholars whose brilliant commentary on the Bible is still studied today. Forced to flee Christian Spain, he journeyed to the Holy Land, and finally entered Jerusalem in 1267 – only to discover a deserted city in shambles.

In a letter to his son describing the poor conditions throughout the land, he wrote: "Many are its forsaken places, and great is the desecration. The more sacred the place, the greater the devastation it has suffered. Jerusalem is the most desolate place of all."

Seeing the holiest city in ruins would seemingly send this great Jewish leader into despondency. Instead, this thirteenth-century scholar recognized the desolation to be a fulfillment of God's promise in the Bible – a hidden blessing – that the land was waiting for the Jews to come back. He pointed to the verses in Leviticus (26:32–33) that describe the land of Israel during exile: "I will make the land desolate; so that your enemies who live in it shall be appalled by it. And I will scatter you among the nations, and I will draw out the sword after you; and your land will be desolate, and your cities will be a waste."

Commenting on this verse, Nachmanides writes that the barren land actually "constitutes a good tiding, proclaiming that during all our exiles, our land will not accept our enemies. This is a great proof and assurance to us," he explains, "for since the time that we left it, [the land] has not accepted any nation or people, and they all try to settle it, but to no avail."

Based on the Bible, Nachmanides foresaw that Israel would remain a wasteland during the many centuries of exile until the Jewish people returned. Then God would once again cause the land to blossom.

Indeed, when the Jewish people began returning to Israel, they encountered a wasteland that had become a malaria-ridden swamp. The new immigrants began to raise funds internationally for trees to soak up the wetlands. Slowly but surely the land was repaired, and the prophecies about Israel began to be fulfilled. "In days to come Jacob will take root, Israel will blossom and bud; and they will fill the face of the world with fruit" (Isaiah 27:6).

Covering the face of the world with fruit is another phrase that in previous years was perhaps unfathomable. But after the Jews resettled the land, agricultural wonders began to abound. For decades, farmers in Israel struggled to grow crops in the arid desert climate. Much of the terrain was dry soil and sand. These harsh conditions forced Israeli farmers to innovate and come up with new ideas, the most famous of which is the Israeli invention of drip irrigation technology.

Engineer Simcha Blass designed a pipe that would drip water onto crops, making it possible to grow them with a limited amount of water. The Jewish state was then able to grow fruits, vegetables, and flowers in the sand. The technology soon spread around the world. Today, Netafim produces and distributes these crop-management technologies in 110 countries and has revitalized more than ten million hectares of land. They have graciously given this drip irrigation technology and training to starving populations in Africa, allowing them to also grow fruits and vegetables and flowers in the sand. In fact, due to Israeli drip irrigation, Kenya is the world's fourth-largest flower exporter. Israeli flowers are exported all over the world, mainly to the Netherlands, one of the market leaders for cut flowers.

Having fresh drinking water is a basic human biological need, yet obtaining that water is difficult in certain regions. Though roughly 71 percent of the Earth's surface is covered in water, less than 1 percent of the drinkable water is available to us, with the rest hidden in glaciers or deep underground. Founded in 2009, the Israeli company Watergen invented technology that can extract humidity directly from the atmosphere everywhere, from rain forests to desert climates. This low-cost solution for creating a renewable source of fresh and clean drinking water has been used in disaster zones. The company now aims to provide clean drinking water for billions of people across the globe, improving quality of life and health.

Israel is also at the cutting edge of desalination, the process of separating salts from water, providing even more people with access to safe clean drinking water. Today, through some of the largest desalination plants in the world, more than 60 percent of Israel's drinking water comes from the ocean.

Another global challenge is dramatic climate change. To address this problem, an Israeli company called SupPlant developed an autonomous irrigation system that analyzes the weather forecast and other data collected by sensors on the ground, and feeds crops according to that data. It also notifies farmers about the ongoing status of their crops, identifying changes in the soil and air within a given plot of land. This technology has helped farmers to significantly reduce their expenditure on water and has increased their yields by 5 percent on average. Some fruits from Israel have three yields a year instead of one – and the produce itself is bigger.

Innovative agricultural technology has also led to the development of some of the world's more popular new fruits and vegetables.[2] For decades, Israeli agricultural experts have brought new fruit and vegetable varieties to the global market. In fact, there are more Israel-developed types of fruits and vegetables growing abroad than in the land of Israel. The Orangetti spaghetti squash, for example, was the first hybrid Israeli vegetable. The mini basil tree, a novel solution to the problem of this herb's naturally short shelf life, can grow outdoors in the summer and be transported indoors during cold weather.

The Israeli company Origene Seeds recently developed a unique seedless type of watermelon with many advantages. This large, round fruit with deep-red flesh, sweet flavor, and longer shelf life produces better yields per hectare and reduces cultivation costs. Cluster (truss) tomatoes, well known throughout the world, were made possible by the introduction of shelf life–extending genes from a group of scientists at Hebrew University. This research group has also enabled other advances, including sweeter and longer-lasting cherry tomatoes.

The healing of the land has also made Israel a prime location for winemaking, a particularly meaningful development for Jews. Wine is not only featured in biblical passages but also used in Jewish sacred ceremonies and traditional rituals for important blessings, such as the sanctification of the Sabbath. Wine was even used as part of the service in the Holy Temple. But seventy years ago, this desolate land had no vineyards. Nevertheless, the Jewish people were destined to once again plant vines, just as they had done in biblical times, and to enjoy the fruits of their labor. "Again you shall plant vineyards on the mountains of Samaria; the planters shall plant and enjoy [the fruit]" (Jeremiah 31:4).

Today, Israel produces some of the best-quality wine on the planet. The challenging landscape has made for a unique terroir, producing interesting flavors. Wineries in Israel work with technological crews and consultants, and have even drilled into solid rock to plant their seeds, forcing the vines to grow deep into the earth for fortifying minerals. Ideas for new blends continue to emerge from wineries made up of inspired people who want to produce something novel and intriguing for their customers.

At the same time, the production of high-quality wines all around Israel is also a way of retracing their roots: restoring ancient Jewish winemaking practices and connecting to the legendary past by setting up vineyards in key biblical sites. Researchers at Ariel University, for example, recently used DNA testing to find a specific type of grape that enabled them to re-create what they believe are the wines consumed during the period of King David and Solomon, and at the Temple in Jerusalem.

These projects have met with extraordinary success. In blind taste tests in France, for example, wine from Israel has won wine-tasting competitions. This is quite an accomplishment considering France has been examining vines for thousands of years – using all the nation's resources to yield the best grape that produces the finest wine – and even has universities that teach on this subject. Yet within just a few decades, Israel has gone from nothing to becoming champions at wine-tasting competitions.

So not only have the deserts bloomed in Israel, but the country produces some of the best fruits, vegetables, flowers, and wines on the planet.

A Light unto the Nations

For many, the celebrated phrase "a light unto the nations" suggests a nation apart, a feeling of pride and responsibility to demonstrate – through devotion to a strict moral code – how people should act. In this sense, Israel tries to be an example of how to best serve God: "And He said, 'It is too small a thing that you should be My servant to raise up the tribes of Jacob and to restore the offspring of Israel; I will also make you a light of the nations, that My salvation may be until the end of the Earth'" (Isaiah 49:6).

This prophecy is an assurance to the Jewish people that God will restore them to the land of Israel, and this return will cause the rest of the world to open their eyes and look up to the people of Israel. This idea also directly connects to Zechariah's prophecy that the nations of the world would look to the Jewish people to show them the way of the One God.

> Many peoples and mighty nations shall come to seek the Lord of Hosts in Jerusalem and to entreat the favor of the Lord. Thus says the Lord of Hosts: In those days it shall come to pass that ten men from all the languages of the nations will take hold of the skirt of a Jew, saying: "We will go with you, for we have heard that God is with you." (Zechariah 8:22–23)

Feeling a sense of responsibility to set a moral example for the world, implementing the vision of the prophet to be a "light unto the nations," is something the United States has emulated from its founding until today. The Puritans applied it in a religious context, possessing a firm conviction that their new country would become a light unto the nations. In February 2018, President Donald Trump referred to the United States as a "light to all nations" at the National Prayer Breakfast.

But there are additional implications and meanings to being "a light unto the nations" – such as through contributions that positively impact the world. Certain Jewish leaders viewed the national revival as a chance to fulfill these prophecies of being a light unto the nations, not simply by abiding by a moral code but through contributing. In his 2017 UN speech, Israeli Prime Minister Benjamin Netanyahu quoted Isaiah that Israel is "a light unto the nations, bringing salvation to the ends of the Earth."

Salvation comes in many forms, from medical innovations to technology that enhances the quality of life. Usually, the larger and wealthier a country is, the more contributions it can make. But to better appreciate how Israel has exemplified the idea of being a light unto the nations, one must understand that the country is no bigger than the size of New Jersey. At the same time, it has developed many of the major technological advances we take for granted in the twenty-first century.

Today, the ten biggest tech companies in the world have research and development centers in Israel. Whereas many countries export natural resources, a large portion of Israel's exports are ideas – most of the exports are technology. The country's greatest resource, in other words, is the number of talented people inspired to share their discoveries with the world.

Over the past twenty years, Israel has become a global technology center, often referred to as the "start-up" nation. In fact, the country has more high-tech start-ups per capita than anywhere else, second only to the US in venture capital funds. For a country just seventy years old, with under nine million people, that is an astonishing achievement. Furthermore, the technology emerging from Israel in a variety of fields has been used to transform people's lives.

Before the invention of the Pentium chip that allows a laptop to be carried around, a desktop was needed – otherwise, it would overheat. The chip that enabled that possibility was developed in Israel. Today, Israel is the second-largest producer of computer chips in the world outside of America.

The first-ever fully viable commercial firewall was developed by an Israeli company, Check Point Software Technologies, in 1993. Another Israeli-based company filed a patent that paved the way for the portable USB drive. Twenty percent of all investments in cybersecurity are in Israel. The ICQ platform that led to text messaging, increasingly the most common form of communication using phones, was developed in Israel.

Collaboration among different disciplines in Israel, such as experts in the medical field together with engineers and scientists, has led to several exciting contributions: Israel developed the PillCam, a swallowable, disposable camera that transmits data to a receiver outside the body and could eventually replace the colonoscopy, is currently being used across the globe to diagnose infections, intestinal disorders, and cancers. Israeli professor Hossam Haick of the Technion–Israel Institute of Technology invented the mobile SniffPhone, a handheld diagnostic device that is able to detect symptomatic odors caused by various diseases from a person's exhaled breath.[3]

Israel has also made vital contributions to nanoscience, the manipulation of individual atoms and molecules, developing technology that can be applied to many fields, such as chemistry, biological sciences, and engineering, in a way that can drastically improve health and save lives. The Center for Nanoscience and Nanotechnology at Tel Aviv University, for example, has grown to ninety research teams that have published nearly two thousand papers and registered two hundred patents. With the use of nanotechnology, scientists are better able to treat disease, prevent illnesses, and diagnose health issues quicker. In order to target specific cancer cells, they need to engineer nanoparticles that encapsulate genetic information.

Engineers have already developed nanobots, tiny ultrasound-powered robots, that can swim through our blood, traveling inside us on a molecular level, to protect the biological system. They can remove harmful bacteria and toxins. DNA robots are now being tested in the body to seek out cancer cells, home in on those cells, and destroy them. They can send an email to a patient from the nanobot, explaining what has happened and informing the patient how to monitor it.

The huge opioid and other addictive medication crises around the world are being treated by a technology developed by BrainsWay, an Israeli company that uses electrodes to stimulate parts of the brain. This revolutionary technology also offers a safe and noninvasive treatment to treat depression and obsessive-compulsive disorder, transforming people's lives.

Every year, roughly 1.3 million people die in car accidents worldwide, with thousands of deaths per day. Coming up with new safety features for vehicles is, therefore, one of Israel's most significant contributions. An Israeli company called Mobileye developed algorithms that allow a tiny camera in cars to alert drivers of potential hazards. Over fifteen million vehicles worldwide are now equipped with the EyeQ technology, keeping drivers safer and preventing serious accidents.

It is often said that time is our most precious resource. Finding ways to save and maximize time can enhance every aspect of one's personal life. An Israeli engineer who investigated GPS systems found that none provide traffic information in real time. So in 2006, he developed an application for road navigation, called Waze, that in addition to guiding drivers to their destination also provides current reports of traffic, accidents, speed traps, and roadwork.

A new era of science and technology is emerging from Israel, while investments to promote more growth are flowing in. Through these breakthroughs, Israel has in multiple ways become a light unto the nations, fulfilling the prophecy.

Jerusalem Will Become a Blessing

In addition to the fulfillment of prophecies about the miraculous development of the land and the Jewish people becoming a light unto the nations, there are prophecies that speak specifically about the city of Jerusalem after the Jewish people return there. Both Jeremiah and Isaiah proclaimed that Jerusalem would be praised across the globe and that the Jewish people would, once again, thrive in their Holy City. "So said the Lord of Hosts: Old men and old women shall yet sit in the streets of Jerusalem, every man with his staff in his hand because of old age. And the streets of the city shall be full of boys and girls playing in its streets" (Zechariah 8:4–5).

What, one might wonder, is so significant about children playing in the streets of Jerusalem? From 1948 until 1967, Jerusalem was desolate, with a relatively tiny population – and it was dangerous. During that period, someone walking down the street into the center of town could be shot by Jordanian snipers from the Old City. It certainly wasn't an area fit for children to be playing.

Only once the Jewish people gained control of the entire city did Jerusalem become a place where children could once again wander safely through the ancient streets. Today, a twelve-year-old girl can walk through Kikar Zion (the main square in downtown Jerusalem) in the middle of the night and feel completely safe. Kidnappings, rapes, and other violent crimes are virtually nonexistent. There is no misuse of guns. Foreigners who visit Jerusalem are often surprised to see the city center bursting with children enjoying their freedom in our Holy City. And mothers can witness the miraculous fulfillment of a prophecy every time they watch their children play ball with friends.

One doesn't have to be a Bible scholar to recognize how God is fulfilling his prophecy in Israel – they just need to pick up the newspaper. As Jews and Christians who believe in the Bible begin to see many prophecies unfolding, they can witness yet another prophecy: the coming together of Jews and Christians in Jerusalem after two thousand years.

CHAPTER 4

The People of the Book

While Judaism and Christianity have obvious points of divergence that define their religions, they share some common beliefs and values that are derived from the Bible. The first basic notion accepted by both faiths is that the world was created out of nothing by an infinite God who established a covenant with Abraham and his descendants. The formal revelation of the desired path for humanity was then given in the Torah to the people of Israel on Mount Sinai.

Sacred Jewish scriptures consist of three main texts: the Five Books of Moses, the Prophets, and the Writings (such as Psalms and Proverbs), collectively known as the Tanach. Within these works are prophecies relating to the exile of the Jewish people from their God-given home, the land of Israel, and their eventual return there. Today, Jewish and Christian groups point to what is happening in Israel as evidence of God's existence, proof that the Bible is an accurate book – historically, archaeologically, and spiritually. As a result of these common beliefs, Jews and Christians from around the world are now joining to support Israel in an unprecedented burst of activity.

This outpouring of support is taking place wherever Bible-believing Christianity thrives. In other words, it is Christians, not countries, who are standing with Israel. And the more Bible-believing Christians there are in a nation, the greater the support for Israel and the Jewish people.

During the Second Intifada, Israeli civilians were targeted by Palestinian suicide bombers, rock attacks, gunfire, and terrorist attacks. One by one, nations began turning against Israel, condemning the Jewish state for defending itself against ruthless Islamic terrorists trying to kill innocent civilians. But despite the mounting pressure from world powers, many Christians stood their ground and supported Israel. They traveled to Israel to show support, even when tourism was at its lowest.

Now, to stand with Israel is never easy. For anyone with an economic agenda, it's not advantageous to support Israel, which has no oil. And while Israel now has natural gas, its wealth and resources are relatively minuscule compared to the surrounding countries. If the US cared *only* about oil and wealth, it would instead support other nations in the Middle East.

The same disadvantage applies to anyone with a political agenda, because standing with Israel is so unpopular. There are twenty-two Arab votes at the United Nations, along with many more Muslim countries who influence other countries, many of whom don't care much about the region, to stand against Israel. Israel, on the other hand, has only one vote. Most of these countries represented at the United Nations are dictatorships and naturally choose to align with similar regimes rather than with the sole democracy in the region. A common visual image given to help portray the giant landmass of all twenty-two Arab countries relative to the land of Israel is a matchbox situated on a football field. The same idea applies to international political weight. In any international forum, therefore, siding with Israel is always going to pose a disadvantage.

Only those people who put their values and beliefs ahead of any economic and political concerns choose to consistently stand with Israel. And when the Israeli leaders noticed the unwavering support by Christian groups, they began to ask themselves: *Why are these Christians standing with Israel while no one else will?*

What the leadership in Israel began to understand was that this support was coming specifically from Bible-believing Christians – not countries – who were expressing their faith in political action. At that point, the Israeli leadership realized that something needed to be done to channel that positive spirit.

The Knesset Christian Allies Caucus

In January 2004, Dr. Yuri Stern – a member of Knesset – and I established the Knesset Christian Allies Caucus within the legislature of the State of Israel. The Christian Allies Caucus aimed to build direct lines of communication to strengthen cooperation and coordination between the leaders of Israel in parliament and Christian leaders around the world – church leaders, heads of organizations, and politicians. Everyone involved sensed that the time had come for Jews and Christians to begin working together in an official capacity to defend God's covenant with Abraham.

But no one knew how this initiative would unfold, or how great the response from the international Christian community would be. There was also hesitation within the Knesset itself about creating such a caucus. At first, it wasn't a popular idea. The religious members of Knesset were wary because they thought it might open Israel to missionary activity. Secular members of the Knesset didn't want a Christian Allies Caucus, since they promote separation between church and state, religion and politics. The right-wing parties didn't like the idea because it seemed to pigeon-hole them as being too right-wing. And the left wing didn't want it either – they thought it was too conservative in policy.

Those proposing the parliamentary action realized its importance, and by borrowing an idea from the US system, they successfully created Israel's first caucus. Before the creation of the KCAC, the Knesset had only lobbies. Lobbies have outside groups pressuring legislatures for action, whereas caucuses are made up only of the members of Parliament who wish to focus on a specific issue. By limiting participation to members of Knesset and focusing on how to develop closer ties with Christians around the world, the KCAC made an immediate impact.

At the first meeting of the KCAC, Reuven Rivlin, who was Speaker of the Knesset at the time, stated that "Jews and Christians need to unite because there are over two billion Christians and thirteen million Jews. But together, we are two billion and thirteen million." Furthermore, he said that if Christians *are* actually going to stand with Israel and become active in helping Israel, they should do it in partnership with the people of Israel.

The Knesset Christian Allies Caucus was ultimately established by members of eight political parties, from the left to the right, religious as well as secular members, reflecting the diversity of the Israeli electorate. At the inaugural meeting, the caucus members pledged to assist Christian organizations with their local Israeli operations and to acquaint fellow members of the Knesset with the pro-Israel work of Christians around the world.

The KCAC began with monthly meetings, discussing various issues while trying to build trust on both sides. These meetings allowed Israeli members of the Knesset to put aside their political differences and find common ground – not just with each other but also with Christian leaders with whom they had never worked. The Israeli Knesset members were inspired by these Christians who recognized that their faith connected them to the Jewish people and the land of Israel. Together, the two groups focused on how to build a strong political alliance, marking the starting point of the idea to take biblical support for Israel and turn it into real political action.

The KCAC began working to further develop relationships between Jews and Christians in the twenty-first century and was wildly successful. This movement came to be known as "faith-based diplomacy."

Two years later, in 2006, something incredible happened. Members of Congress in Washington, DC, inspired by the work of the Knesset Christian Allies Caucus, decided to start the first sister caucus in the House of Representatives. The Congressional Israel Allies Caucus was established by cochairs Dr. David Weldon, a Christian Republican, and Eliot Engel, a Jewish Democrat. Its members are Republicans and Democrats, Jews and Christians, who work together to mobilize support for Israel. It is the only bipartisan caucus on Capitol Hill working on behalf of Israel.

This caucus in Washington prompted a domino effect of other countries joining the movement and starting caucuses in their respective governments. First, the Canadian Parliamentary Israel Allies Caucus was formed, followed by a caucus in Latin America, and then in Europe. Today, there are over forty caucuses: one each in Israel, the United States, and Canada, fourteen in Europe, eleven in Africa, nine in Latin America, three in Asia, and one in Australia and Papua New Guinea. Consisting altogether of about a thousand members elected to their parliaments, these caucuses work as a network to mobilize political support for Israel.

The secret ingredient in this faith-based diplomacy has been grassroots Christian supporters who encourage their pastors to speak to their political representatives about why, as Christians who believe in the Bible, it's important to support the State of Israel. This enthusiastic effort led to the establishment of the Israel Allies Foundation in 2007. The foundation's aim was to coordinate the activities of all the Israel Allies Caucuses around the world on specific initiatives.

The foundation's initial areas of focus were (1) fighting the anti-Semitic boycott, divestment, and sanctions movement; (2) fighting the threat of Iran; and (3) recognizing Jerusalem as the undivided capital of the State of Israel. These three initiatives were important to Bible-believing Christians, and we were able, at the grassroots level, to create a big surge of international support.

Within the American political system, there's always been a strong group of people who support Israel: evangelical Christians and representatives in the Republican Party have generally been friendly toward Israel. One reason for this allegiance is that it would be difficult for any Republican to be elected to the House, or the Senate, or the presidency, without evangelical Christian support. And from the beginning of Israel's establishment in 1948, these Christians have faithfully embraced Israel as an ally. Many important evangelical leaders – such as Pat Robertson, Jerry Falwell, and Billy Graham – publicly and passionately expressed their endorsement of the Jewish state.

Evangelical Christians' stance on Israel has long been a critical issue in the Republican Party, as many Republican representatives realize that Israel is extremely important to their conservative constituents. On the other side of the political equation, the Democratic Party needs to show support for Israel because a significant amount of funding comes from the American Jewish community.

Unfortunately, everything changed during the Obama administration. Former President Barack Obama was the first American leader to go against this foundational component of standing with Israel and openly work against the interests of Israel, while still retaining American Jewish support. This major diversion caused a rift within the Democratic American Jewish community, forcing them to choose between liberal values or support for the Jewish state. But while the Jewish Democrats wavered, evangelical Christian support for Israel became even more important and influential.

The Success of Faith-Based Diplomacy

Faith-based diplomacy, within the last few years, has created some of the most impressive successes in the history of US-Israel relations. The first big accomplishment was the passage of legislation against the boycott, divestment, and sanctions (BDS) movement. The anti-BDS legislation began with a grassroots movement, sparked by churches speaking to state representatives.

The effort began in South Carolina in June 2015. South Carolina, in the heart of the South, has a small Jewish population. Yet it was the Bible-believing Christians with their love for Israel who sparked the movement. Alan Clemmons, a member of the state's House of Representatives, initiated the first anti-BDS bill. South Carolina then passed a historic law that banned the state from entering contracts with companies participating in boycotts "based on race, color, religion, gender, or national origin."

This meant that any company that boycotted Israel was viewed as discriminatory and therefore could not do business with the state in which that company operated. The passing of this law – an initiative inspired by people in churches who talked to their pastors and prompted their state senators – was a major blow to the anti-Semitic attempts of the BDS movement. Similar legislation spread to twenty-seven states, now including New York, Texas, and Florida. The new rules represented a potential loss of $3.5 trillion for any company that was involved in the BDS movement. Now, what company would want to risk losing that amount of money?

This effective initiative to block the anti-Semitic campaign through legislation – driven by faith-based diplomacy – was particularly significant, because five years ago BDS posed one of the biggest strategic threats to the State of Israel. The idea behind the movement was that if Israel could not be defeated militarily, then its economy would be attacked, thereby crippling the country.

This international effort to harm Israel, backed by vicious anti-Semites and terror organizations, managed to put pressure on major corporations. BDS coordinators delivered the message that any company wanting to do business with the numerous and powerful Arab states would need to cease working with the single Jewish state they opposed. If successful, that scheme would have caused a major setback to the Israeli economy.

But when state governments in the United States stood up and began passing laws stating they would not do business with companies boycotting Israel, many corporations backed off. This response to the BDS movement highlights how influential faith-based diplomacy can be – and it stemmed directly from the Christian grassroots desire to protect Israel.

Another example coming through the pipeline is anti-Semitism legislation, which has recently passed in South Carolina and Florida.

The US State Department equates anti-Zionism to anti-Semitism, but this interpretation hasn't yet been made into a federal law or state law. This has enormous effects on university campuses and institutions, which often try hard to demonize Israel. It also paved the way for President Trump's courageous decision to issue a presidential decree combating anti-Semitism throughout the US by executive order in December 2019 – a huge setback to anti-Semitic activity on university campuses across America.

But by far the biggest success in the short history of faith-based diplomacy was the relocation of the US embassy from Tel Aviv to the Israeli capital of Jerusalem in 2018. This decision marked the long-awaited implementation of the Jerusalem Embassy Act of 1995. The decades-long delay was due to the repeated use of a presidential waiver, meaning that every sitting president since 1995 signed a waiver every six months, effectively stalling the implementation of the law that required the United States embassy to move to Jerusalem.

The recent enactment of the new Republican platform and the promise Trump made to his Christian supporters to move the embassy removed that obstacle and increased momentum toward relocating the United States embassy. Until then, the embassy move was largely perceived as an issue pushed by segments of the Jewish community. Then, it became a major issue for Bible-believing Christians, who made this embassy move one of the conditions under which they would support Trump.

When President Trump took the bold step to move the embassy, he sent a clear message to the world that Jerusalem is undeniably the capital of Israel. Many of Trump's Christian supporters were ecstatic. They applauded the administration for being a great friend to the Jewish people. Trump had kept his campaign promise and rectified a twenty-three-year-long injustice. This Christian support was most visible at the ceremony at the new embassy site, where out of the eight hundred people invited to Jerusalem, seven hundred were evangelical Christians, mostly pastors from across America. And for the first time, this act was recognized as a Christian concern as well as a Jewish one.

Sweeping the Nations

Faith-based diplomacy is not only succeeding in America, it's spreading across the globe. In Africa, there is a group of nations standing with Israel, as a Christian bloc, for the first time. Eastern European countries are coming out, as never before, against BDS – all because of the work of key Bible-believing members of parliament in their countries. There has also been a recent shift in Latin America. Christian countries such as Guatemala, for example, moved their embassies to Jerusalem. Paraguay moved its embassy out of Tel Aviv to Jerusalem, though it was later moved back under the new president, Mario Abdo Benítez. Brazil and Honduras have recently announced the establishment of trade offices in Jerusalem to increase economic cooperation between the countries; both stated plans to move their embassies there as well.

What all these nations have in common is a massive population of Bible-believing Christians who are speaking out and persuading their leaders to support the Jewish state. In effect, where there are Bible-believing Christians, there is a new and unprecedented wave of support for Israel. Faith-based diplomacy has become the most effective weapon in Israel's diplomatic arsenal.

In America, this governmental support is more developed because there's already a well-established political party backed by Bible-believing Christians who believe that God has given them a duty to support Israel. Candidates have responded to these beliefs by pushing a pro-Israel agenda. In other countries around the

world, however, there isn't a government party in which evangelicals come together.

But now, people in these countries are also starting to vote for
and support candidates who are pro-Israel, just like in America.
So although America was a pioneer in this type of movement, we
can now see it happening in Latin American countries, Eastern
European countries, and African countries. Evangelicals are uniting under political banners and using their support to push a
more pro-Israel agenda.

This new movement of faith-based diplomacy is only going
to strengthen in years to come, as more people are willing to take
their biblical beliefs – their support for Israel – and turn it into
real political action.

Spiritual Cooperation

Alongside the political support for Israel from Christians all over
the world, there has also been spiritual cooperation. In 2004, a
movement began to establish a new holiday in the Christian calendar called the Day of Prayer for the Peace of Jerusalem. Today,
millions of Christians around the world conduct prayer meetings for Jerusalem on the first Sunday of every October because
they believe they are obligated, according to scripture, to support
and pray for the State of Israel. "Pray for the peace of Jerusalem;
may those who love you prosper. May there be peace within your
walls, prosperity within your palaces" (Psalms 122:6–7).

These Christians recognize that their belief in the Bible connects them to the land and the people of Israel. Their intention
during these prayer meetings involves the idea that Jerusalem –
under the Jewish leadership and Jewish sovereignty – should
be protected. Jews began joining with Christians on this day to

participate in praying for the peace of Jerusalem. Since this prayer is taken from the book of Psalms, it allows Jews to also embrace the content.

Christian groups around the world, from Sierra Leone to South Korea, pray day and night for the leadership of Israel, the people of Israel, for peace and security in the land of Israel. As part of this spiritual cooperation, Jewish spiritual leaders began offering Bible studies, specifically designed to teach non-Jews the basic principles of Judaism. At the same time, pastors such as Larry Huch and John Hagee in Texas encourage their congregants to explore their Jewish roots and learn about the biblical Jewish festivals. There is also a movement of Christian churches, thousands of them across America, who now conduct Passover Seders. All these activities are part of a global movement by Christians to discover the origins of their religion by adopting biblical feasts and holidays as part of their practice.

In conjunction with increased communication and cooperation between Jews and Christians for political purposes, we're also witnessing a spiritual awakening that recognizes the importance of Judaism in the lives of Christians.

For the above reasons, Christians are hungry to learn all they can about Israel, from its holy sites to activities taking place in the land. And they now look outside of mainstream media to report the news from Israel: Daystar, TBN (Trinity Broadcasting Network), and God TV are Christian television networks that are available full time on basic cable and satellite around the world. These networks are committed to supporting the country and people of Israel, providing updates from Israel, and interviewing important people about the land.

The International Christian Embassy Jerusalem hosts the largest annual Christian tourist event in Israel, in which thousands of

Christians from a hundred countries participate during the Jewish festival of Sukkot, commonly known as the Feast of Tabernacles. These devoted Christians can be seen marching in the streets of Jerusalem, waving Israeli flags to show support for the Jewish state. The International Christian Embassy Jerusalem was given this name, despite opposition from other international groups, to express its acknowledgment of the biblical significance of all of Jerusalem and its distinct connection to the Jewish people.

The All Nations Convocation brings thousands of Christians from around the world to Israel during the Days of Awe – the calendar period from Rosh Hashanah through Yom Kippur – to pray for Israel. Another organization, Bridges for Peace, considers it their mission to support Israel and the Jewish people. As part of this mission, they offer programs in Israel and around the world in which Christians can build relationships with Jews and expressing their Biblical responsibility through volunteer services and by helping to counter anti-Semitism. Bridges for Peace operates the largest food bank in Israel, providing thousands of tons of food for the needy.

These types of organizations are steadily growing each year as Christians begin to understand that an important part of being a Christian is to learn the Hebrew Bible and to be a part of the fulfillment of prophecy. This also leads to organizations supporting aliyah, the emigration of Jews to Israel, which is seen as a vital stage in the ingathering of the exiles.

Other philanthropic organizations uniting Jews and Christians pour tens of millions of dollars in financial aid to help assist people in Israel. For example, the International Fellowship of Christians and Jews, founded by Rabbi Yechiel Eckstein to support Jews in need of financial help, currently raises more than $160 million annually from Christian donors.

The burst of political activity and spiritual cooperation is coming to a head all at the same time, making faith-based diplomacy increasingly stronger. People at the top echelons are involved. One of the cochairpersons of the Congressional Israel Allies Caucus was Mike Pence, now the vice president of the United States.

As faith-based diplomacy grows stronger around the world, so does spiritual cooperation and financial cooperation. As a result, Christian tourism to Israel breaks records every year. There's never been more active support from Christians flowing toward Israel, through coming to Israel, investing in Israel, providing financial and political support for Israel, and praying for Israel.

All this activity is because Christians are realizing that God is continuing to fulfill prophecies in Israel. For many Christians, this is the most exciting story in their lifetime. The people who believed in the Bible all these years can now point to Israel and say, *Look, what we believe is true. The God of Israel is real. The Bible is not only historically accurate but also an accurate predictor of the future – and that's why we are standing with Israel.*

This recognition by the Christian people is changing the way countries stand with Israel. We can now look to Africa and Latin America and Asia and Eastern Europe and see a new, vibrant flow of support and independent activity cropping up in these countries, all because of the rise of evangelical Bible-believing Christianity.

This movement has had a profound effect on Christianity as a whole. Brazil, for example, was predominantly Catholic in 1948. Today, it is 35 percent Bible-believing Christian, which amounts to sixty million Bible-believing Christians in Brazil alone. The way evangelicals won over their followers is by pointing to Israel and asking: *How can you still believe in replacement theology? How can you believe that you replaced Jews, or that Rome replaced Jerusalem, when it's clear that God is fulfilling his covenant with Israel and rebuilding Jerusalem right before your very eyes?*

What's Behind This Change in Attitude?

From a historical perspective, Christianity has changed its stance toward Jews. Former governor Sam Brownback of Kansas, who in 2018 became the US ambassador-at-large for international religious freedom, once made a statement that Christians and Jews are like two groups walking up the same mountain from different sides who are just now reaching the top and starting to see each other. The alliance between Jews and Christians, he explained, has always existed in potential, but it was previously done independently and sometimes with disdain for one another. One factor for this separation is that the Jewish mandate has always been to serve as a light unto other nations, to lead by example: "You are a holy people to the Lord, your God, and the Lord has chosen you to be His own treasure out of all peoples that are upon the face of the Earth" (Deuteronomy 14:2).

Part of that mandate meant that Jews were to remain set apart from other nations. The Jewish task was to show, through action, how one is supposed to be a good person. Many Christians, on the other hand, believed they were commanded to go out and spread their beliefs through conversion.

While the Jews were focusing on their specific mission – to observe the commandments, keep their traditions, and lead by example – Christians were traveling around the world and spreading their messages from scripture. An outcome of this missionary activity over the years is that there are now said to be twenty million evangelical Christians in the Philippines who stand with Israel. This support isn't due to a group of rabbis who went there and educated the masses about the spiritual significance of Israel (or the covenant with the people of Israel) – it's because Christian missionaries taught them the Bible.

In 1948, there were only six million Bible-believing Christians. They traveled around the world, persuading people to believe in what they believed. They pointed to the return of the Jewish people to their land, the ingathering of the exiles, the deserts blooming, the people of Israel becoming a light unto the nations, the crowds coming to visit Israel, and the fulfillment of the verse that speaks about children playing in the streets of Jerusalem.

Linking these events to ancient prophecies (mentioned in chapter three) helped to convince people within other branches in Christianity, such as Catholics and Anglicans, that they had erred from a theological perspective. Despite what they had been taught, the covenant never left the Jewish people, and consequently, they too should become Bible-believing Christians who support Israel. The Bible-believing Christians also explained how they, as the minority of Christians who stood with Israel, had been right all along. They used these arguments to fortify their numbers, growing from six million evangelical Bible-believing Christians to six hundred million in just seventy years.

Today, for the first time in our generation, the paths of Jews and Christians are coinciding. Although Christianity was often a curse to the Jewish people over the centuries, responsible for vilifying, persecuting, and advocating violence toward Jews, this same religion is now a blessing. More Christians are beginning to view their faith through the eyes of the Hebrew Bible and are turning away from replacement theology.

From Africa to Asia to Latin America, people are saying, *God is standing up for the Jews and fulfilling his promise. We need to stand with Israel and support these people, not persecute them. God's covenant with them is an* everlasting *covenant – and we want to be a part of it.*

It's not only a question of independent church leaders, reflecting on their past and the history of violence and cruelty to Jews, calling for repentance and a new approach. Nor is it a revision of their interpretation of the scriptures that has garnered this support for Israel. Rather, it's what they have witnessed in Israel that prompted them to revisit how they explained scripture.

What lies behind this change in Christian-Jewish relations is also important for Jews to understand. Until now, most Jews, especially those living in Israel, couldn't make sense of the new phenomenon. Many of them observed the recent wave of support and wondered, *Why do some Christians hate us, while other Christians embrace us? What's the difference?*

One role of the Knesset Christian Allies Caucus has been to educate the Israeli public about this Christian support for Israel, and to facilitate a relationship between Christians and Jews everywhere. The sister caucuses have become a forum for cooperation, where groups work together to support both Israel and their local Jewish communities. The Knesset Caucus has likewise sparked a flurry of cooperation between Jews and Christians in Israel.

We are seeing a new, energetic, and close relationship between Jews and Christians in the twenty-first century, something most people thought to be impossible. But as Jews and Christians are coming together because of their common faith in the God of Israel and the Bible, there are also groups around the world uniting because of their resentment for what God is doing in Israel.

PART 2
THE NEW AXIS

CHAPTER 5

The Anti-Semitism Virus

Jews and Christians are coming together around the world to support Israel in an unprecedented burst of activity, inspired by their strong beliefs in the God of Israel and the Bible, as we discussed in part 1, "The Alliance." For the first time in many generations, people don't need to rely on faith alone to proclaim that God is real and the words of the Bible are true – they can see it for themselves. Not only is the Bible an accurate document historically, it's an accurate predictor of the future: prophecies are being fulfilled through the many miracles and blessings in Israel. These two groups are celebrating by working together.

While this is an exciting time for people who believe in the Bible, it is an equally alarming period for those who deny the God of Israel and the Bible. If you don't believe in the Bible, and you don't believe in the covenants mentioned there, how do you explain what's happening in Israel? It doesn't make sense that despite all odds, these people have repeatedly survived the worst persecutions and have now returned to the land of their forefathers to rebuild and restore it to become one of the most advanced, prosperous, and powerful countries in the world – just as it was predicted in their sacred scriptures.

While Jews and Christians are busy uniting to support Israel, the ardent disbelievers of God and the Bible are uniting to oppose Israel with clear disdain and hatred, because they begrudge all the good that is happening there.

Such resentment and hatred for the Jewish people has historically been termed anti-Semitism, an ancient moral virus. Animosity aimed at the Jews has taken different forms and emerged in almost every place where Jews have lived. When sparked, it spreads like wildfire. Many people have speculated about the root cause of anti-Semitism throughout the ages. Though there is no one satisfactory explanation for this essentially irrational behavior, it may be suggested that the seed of all the hostility is the rejection of the God of Israel.

The Roots of Anti-Semitism

The Jewish people have always been regarded as a nation apart, separated by God through their laws of purity, kosher foods, and observing the Sabbath. Jews believe that their call to be a light unto the nations is part of their purpose in this world, their responsibility to lead by example. And because they have historically upheld certain ethics and held strong to their beliefs, refusing to be converted or persuaded despite the extreme determination of other faiths, Jews have been perceived as a threat.

In the ancient world and classical civilizations, anti-Semitism was based on rejecting the idea of one God. The pattern began with Abraham when he walked into his father's store and began breaking Terah's idols, proclaiming there's only one Creator. Seen as a threat by the locals, Abraham was persecuted and forced to flee. In Roman times, people resented the Jewish faith because paganism dominated their world. Since the worship of many gods was part of Roman culture, to be Jewish was, in effect, to suggest that all these people were mistaken.

During this period of classical antiquity, Jews kept separate holy days from the festivals adopted by the conventional culture, they dressed differently, and ate different foods from the rest of the population. And because the Jewish people were constantly standing alone against the popular current, other nations reacted by trying to prove them wrong. Seen in this context, the source of anti-Semitism is the fight against monotheism.

But as other nations became more monotheistic and Christianity and Islam spread, people began to acknowledge monotheism. Anti-Semitism then targeted the Jews for being the specific people that the God of Israel had chosen. The two cultures where enmity appeared most were in the Arab Islamic nations and European Christian countries.

The common theological root that gave rise to repeated anti-Semitic sentiment within Christianity and Islam was the belief that their religion had come into the world to *replace* Judaism. Yet having Jewish residents in their midst, carefully adhering to their Bible, was a constant reminder of the opposite. They detested Jews for not accepting their prophets and scriptures, and for refusing to adopt their faith. As a result, they often sought to humiliate and persecute Jewish citizens in order to demonstrate to themselves that they were part of the true religion and Judaism was wrong.

That's also why in places like China, Japan, and India, where the prevailing religions are disconnected from Judaism – unlike Islam and Christianity, which are derivatives – this anti-Jewish sentiment is absent. People in those cultures never had any underlying motivation to vilify the Jews in order to assert their own validity.

At times, vengeance against the Jewish community expressed itself in laws against eating kosher and adhering to the commandments in the Bible. There were plenty of efforts to convert or physically wipe out the Jewish people. Anti-Semitism because of monotheism changed to a cultural anti-Semitism, a resentment for Jews having a unique identity and refusing to adopt the practices of the surrounding faiths. In the book of Esther (3:8–9), Haman, who sought to annihilate the Jewish people, expresses his plan to the ruler of Persia as follows: "There is a certain people scattered among but separate from the peoples in all the provinces of your kingdom, and their laws differ from those of every people...it is therefore not in the king's interest to let them be. If it pleases the king, let it be written to destroy them."

Later in history, as anti-Semitism spread through Europe, the hatred manifested in economic concerns. Jewish people were not allowed to own land. They were not allowed to farm. These laws severely harmed Jewish communities since, in those days, people acquired wealth through owning and cultivating land to sell produce. Jews were forced to find other means to make money, outside of agriculture. One of those professions became banking. They also pursued cultural activities – playwriting, music, literature, and art – and thrived.

But cultural success posed another threat to the other nations. Even when Jews abandoned their religious distinctions and were completely assimilated, aiding in the economic growth of a country, holding positions in politics, and contributing to the arts and sciences, the worst anti-Semitism still arose – specifically *because* Jews seemed to blend in so well. Once Jews became expert financiers and lawyers, the local population began saying, *Now these*

Jews are trying to take our money and to trick us. Another type of anti-Semitism sprouted: a reminder that, despite all efforts to be accepted as equal citizens, the Jew was still seen as different.

The newest brand of anti-Semitism, and the most prevalent of our time, is anti-Zionism, a movement that ultimately seeks to mask a baseless hatred and deny the Jewish people their right to self-determination in the land of Israel.

If one looks at anti-Semitism in the 1930s and anti-Zionism today, the two oppositions employ the same tactics. In April 1933, soon after the Nazis came to power in Germany, the government sponsored Judenboykott, a nationwide boycott of Jewish shops. The campaign attempted to not only hurt the Jewish community economically but to stigmatize the Jewish people. Later, Jewish businessmen were forced to close their stores or sell them at a fraction of the market value. The efforts continued to drive Jews from the German economy and strip them of their assets.

Today, the boycott, divestment, and sanctions movement uses the same strategy by telling people not to purchase Israeli products, and pressures companies to boycott Israel. In Germany before the war, the anti-Semitic movements rejected Jewish doctors, attorneys, and professors. These days, BDS is trying to eliminate everything that can be considered pro-Israel from universities, pressuring Jewish students on campus to either adhere to this position or face harassment and intimidation. They once again try to ostracize the Jews by advising against hiring Israeli professors, buying from Israeli businesses, and seeing Israeli doctors. All they've done is change the word "Jewish" to "Israeli." It's the old spirit of anti-Semitism garbed in a new style called anti-Zionism.

The anti-Zionist movement is also resuscitating medieval anti-Semitic rhetoric. The blood libels of the 1100s and 1200s in England and Europe claimed that the Jews were murdering Christian children, intending to use their blood to make matzah (Passover bread). After Europe suffered several waves of the Black Death, the poisoning of wells was another grave accusation against the Jews of the late Middle Ages.

Today, Arabs spread the same kind of atrocious lies, claiming the Israeli government targets innocent civilians and even gives poisonous candies to Palestinian children. Suha Arafat, the wife of former Palestinian Authority president Yasser Arafat, propagated similar lies to Hillary Clinton during her 1999 visit to Israel. More recently, in his address to the European Parliament on June 23, 2016, Palestinian president Mahmoud Abbas repeated a widely discredited report accusing rabbis in Israel of demanding that their government poison the water to kill the Palestinians – and received a standing ovation. Abbas later admitted that these allegations were "baseless." All this is a throwback to the old blood libels spread about Jews through the centuries.

Another anti-Semitic idea from the 1930s concerned the wandering Jews, portrayed as people who come into other countries with the goal of controlling their economic systems and taking over the land. The same claim is now thrown around in reference to Israel. In returning to their historic homeland, the Jewish people have been accused of taking over *someone else's* country. The Jewish restoration of the Old City has been spun as the "occupation" of Arab East Jerusalem.

It's clear from the Bible that there are no people with a stronger connection to a land or a capital city than the Jewish people have to the land of Israel and Jerusalem – a connection lasting for thousands of years. Long before Islam and Christianity came to the scene, the Jews were living in Jerusalem worshipping the God of Israel. King David, Solomon, and all the prophets were

Jews. This connection to the land is reflected through the Bible, through history, and through archaeological evidence. The only capital that's ever existed in Jerusalem has been Jewish. Yet when the Jewish people returned to the land of their forefathers, to rebuild the country and reestablish their independence and freedom there, the story spread by the enemies of Israel was a version of the wandering Jew invading another people's land.

The entire concept of a Palestinian identity is a political tool that developed in response to Zionism and is being used against Israel. From 1948 to 1967, Jordan occupied Judea, Samaria, and East Jerusalem, yet nobody – not the Arab League, nor the world powers – pressured Jordan to make a Palestinian state with Jerusalem as its capital. Only after Jerusalem was liberated by the Jews did the protests begin. Along with this resentment for a Jewish state came the promotion of myths surrounding the Palestinian people.

The people who identify as Palestinians try to trace their roots back to the Bible, claiming that they are descendants of the Philistines who appear in many of the Hebrew narratives. The first weak point in their claim relates to the name itself. Contrary to the common narrative, the word "Palestine" is not Arab in origin. In fact, in Arabic you can't even pronounce the word properly, as there's no letter that makes the "P" sound. The country was referred to as Palestine, or Palestina, by the Roman Caesar Hadrian in the second century CE as a means to denigrate the Jews. He intended to disconnect the Jewish people from Jerusalem by renaming Judea after one of the kingdom of Israel's most dangerous enemies in the Hebrew Bible, the Philistines.

The Philistines were a Greek group of Aegean origin who settled on the shore in the twelfth century BCE and frequently fought with the Jews in their land. At some point, they returned to their original location. Archaeological remains indicate that culturally, they were completely Greek. Those who adopt the title of Palestinians today are, in effect, linking themselves to a *Greek* group who once lived on the south coast of Canaan and later left the region. The actual Philistines have no connection to the Arab world.

This tactic of groups adopting the name of an ancient people who lived in the land thousands of years ago for the purpose of proving that they belong there is a common and well-known practice in the Arab Middle East. The Iraqi Arabs, for example, claim that they are the descendants of the Babylonians. Saddam Hussein claimed to have a list of ancestors that goes back to Hammurabi, one of the greatest Babylonian kings. Suddenly someone from the Arabian Peninsula becomes a Babylonian descendant.

The Lebanese claim to descend from the Phoenicians, who lived there before Arabs ever came to the area in the seventh century and conquered and changed the entire landscape. Most Egyptians came from the Arabian Peninsula, invaded Egypt, and exterminated the Christian men. Now they claim to be descendants of the pharaohs who ruled Egypt thousands of years ago. This practice of concocting claims to one's ancestry – despite evidence that the ancestors lived in a different area with another language and culture – is accepted and embedded in Middle Eastern culture as a means of survival.

The practice of occupying not only the land but appropriating the history of the area to gain political credibility also connects to the Bedouin society. After migrating to an inhabited area in search of trees and water, a tribe would pitch their tents at night and plan to take over the land from the current residents. In the morning, when confronted by the locals, they simply claimed – with a straight face – that their ancestors had lived there for thousands of years. The reengineering of history also applies to religion. According to Islam, Abraham was the first Muslim, Jesus was also Muslim, and King Solomon built a *mosque* in Jerusalem.

These days, the groups claiming to be Palestinians are merely a collection of Arabs descended from tribes in Iraq, Yemen, and Syria. Some clans are Kurdish or Egyptian. Historically, there was never a country or people called Palestine. There was never any capital for any Palestinian people in Israel. There was never a Palestinian flag, a Palestinian leader, or king. There was never a Palestinian currency. These Arabs of Palestine have no language, religion, or culture distinct from the Arabs of Syria, Jordan, or other nearby areas. Yet through stories driven by anti-Semitism, they claim that the Jewish people have tried to establish a new country by usurping the natives – that same libel of the wandering Jew.

So just as Hadrian changed the name Judea to Palestine to disconnect Jerusalem from the Jewish people, the modern use of the word Palestine is a device to erase the record of the Jews in the land, to reinvent history, and to deny Jewish rights to the land of Israel despite all the evidence that the only nation who ever ruled that land directly – and not as intruders – was the Jewish people.

A scarf of the Palestinian Liberation Organization has the phrase "Jerusalem Is Ours" printed on one side – a false claim to the land. On the other side, an image of the entire land of "Palestine" is portrayed.[4] Put simply, Jerusalem is only the beginning of their desire to conquer all of Israel. Their slogan "From the river to the sea, Palestine will be free" explicitly refers to the *entire* land of Israel. Jerusalem has come into focus only because the anti-Semitic movement understands the inherent link between Jerusalem and Palestine. They know that if they can take Zion (Jerusalem) away from the Jews, it would be the end of Zionism.

Anti-Zionism Is Anti-Semitism

These days, anti-Zionism has become the shrewdest way to be anti-Semitic. By masking anti-Semitism as anti-Zionism, it is easier to bash Israel in political meetings and more-sophisticated venues. When questioned, anti-Zionists simply respond, "We're not anti-Semitic, we're just anti-Israel." This way, any criticism becomes more acceptable.

One place where anti-Semites converge is on American college campuses. Student organizations join in Israeli Apartheid Week, when they claim Israel is a usurper of land, that the Israeli government is persecuting and murdering Arabs. As angry crowds of students yell out their ill-informed opinions, there is no room for any civil dialogue or rational debate. Jewish students (and professors) are compelled to keep quiet, and those who support Israel – or don't condemn Israel – are threatened and harassed.

It used to be that venomous verbal attacks at these campus events were confined to anti-Israel rhetoric. Lately, however, they have turned into slogans against Jews. On February 10, a meeting of the Associated Students of the University of California (Berkeley) declined to pass a bill condemning a Bears for Palestine tribute to convicted terrorists; one student (who actually identified herself as Jewish) stated, "I stand with the Palestinian freedom fighters acting out of self-defense."[5] In March 2020, Northeastern University Students for Justice in Palestine (SJP) advertised their "Israel Apartheid Week" with a poster depicting Jewish Israelis in a terrorist's gun sights, with kaffiyeh-clad militants brandishing weapons.[6] These declarations promoting bloodshed are thrown around casually on campus and have not even been considered as hate speech, or anti-Semitic, because they pose as political commentary.

Jew-hatred under the guise of anti-Zionism has also spread through Europe. There was a case in Germany, for example, where Arab terrorists bombed a synagogue in 2014. They were acquitted of anti-Semitism because they claimed it was their right to be politically against Israel. Anti-Semitism in Europe has become so mainstream that it no longer hides behind the façade of anti-Zionism. More recently, an annual parade in Aalst, Belgium, featured participants dressed in costumes of Orthodox Jews with gross caricatures – including fake hook noses and insect bodies – as well as displays of grinning Jewish figures holding bags of money. The caricatures appeared in both 2019 and 2020, along with parade participants in Klan costumes one year and Nazi officer garb the next. The mayor of the city, Christoph D'Haese of the right-wing New Flemish Alliance, refused to take any preventive action, claiming that the displays in the carnival were not anti-Semitic, and the parade went forward despite the condemnation of Belgium's prime minister, Sophie Wilmès.

Other politicians in Europe have made active attempts to ban circumcision and kosher slaughtering. They claim it's because the rituals are inhumane, displaying child abuse or animal abuse. But the real force behind these initiatives is an attempt to harm Jewish citizens by keeping them from practicing their religion.

The recent rise of anti-Semitism is, for some, a surprising change – but it shouldn't be. Anti-Semitism has reared its ugly head in every generation. It's only a question of when it happens, who participates, and who stands against it. As columnist Charles Krauthammer said, "The rise of European anti-Semitism is, in reality, just a return to the norm. For a millennium, virulent Jew-hatred – persecution, expulsions, massacres – was the norm in Europe until the shame of the Holocaust created a temporary anomaly wherein anti-Semitism became socially unacceptable."[7]

The surprise is not that anti-Semitism has once again surfaced in Europe; it's that they've been able to keep it under wraps for seventy years.

European politicians are acknowledging the growing problem. In his Chanukah message of 2019, UK prime minister Boris Johnson pledged his commitment to combat anti-Semitism and echoed this idea of latent hatred coming to the surface. "In the media, on the streets, and particularly online, anti-Semites have, in alarming numbers, been emboldened to crawl out from under their rocks and begin, once again, to spread their brand of noxious hatred far and wide," he began.

> But as you kindle the Chanukah light tonight and in the nights to come, I want you to remember this: When the Maccabees drove the forces of darkness out of Jerusalem, they had to do so on their own. Today, as Britain's Jews seek to drive back the darkness of resurgent anti-Semitism, you have every decent person in this country fighting by your side – because Britain would not be Britain without its Jewish community.

Since raw anti-Semitism is more widely viewed as problematic after the Holocaust, the tactic of channeling hatred for Jews through anti-Zionism helps to make it more palatable to the world. There are even those who use historical persecution of Jews to justify why they so fervently attack Israel. Several political leaders in Europe assert that the reason that they are pro-Palestinian is *because of* the Holocaust. In other words, because of what happened to the Jewish people during the Holocaust, we can't allow Palestinian people to be oppressed.

Such comparisons display complete ignorance of both the Holocaust and the current conflict in Israel. The Nazis systematically murdered and attempted to wipe out the Jewish people. The Israeli government, on the other hand, is forced to defend itself from constant threats of terror by the surrounding Arab nations. But rather than deriving an appropriate lesson from the atrocities of the Holocaust – that the Jewish people needed their own state so that they wouldn't be attacked and murdered – some politicians use the suffering of the Jewish people to condemn them, in the name of protecting the Palestinians.

The International Holocaust Remembrance Alliance's definition of anti-Semitism, adopted by several governments and the US State Department, provides examples of anti-Semitic behavior. Included in this is "denying the Jewish people their right to self-determination, e.g., by claiming that the existence of a State of Israel is a racist endeavor... drawing comparisons of contemporary Israeli policy to that of the Nazis" and "holding Jews collectively responsible for the actions of the state of Israel."

Anti-Semitism, even though it has been a long-standing virus throughout the generations, is now being manipulated in the form of promoting anti-Zionism. And these anti-Semitic groups turn to extremely liberal Jews for support and validity. Historically, there have always been those amongst the Jewish community who, even though they were born Jewish, have been motivated to attack the Jewish people from within, once they outwardly rejected God. Trying to ingratiate themselves with a political party, or to demonstrate their impartiality, they join and even lead the fight against their own people. And we're seeing this peculiar and self-destructive behavior again in our times regarding Israel. As Jews and Christians who believe in the Bible come together to support Israel, there's an alliance of people who don't believe in the Bible who stand together as well. Among that alliance are Jews who actively reject God and the Bible.

This hatred of the Jewish people and of Israel stemming from a rejection of God has also played out in other areas. As Bible-believing Christianity grows around the world, based on the idea that they're grafted into the covenant with the Jewish people, there has been backlash against the Christian community. Politicians try to pass laws forbidding the mention of God or the Bible or the Ten Commandments in public places.

This irrational hatred toward Jews and Bible-believing Christians is also a big cause of irrational anti-Trump sentiment. While previously, people were against Obama's policy in the Middle East or against the deal he was pushing with Iran, they were not as quick to claim that Obama was an anti-Semite or the root of all evil. Yet the current president is being attacked from all sides. On one side, there's a large group of people who criticize Trump for being too pro-Jewish, such as David Duke, who claimed that the president is a pawn of Israel. Likewise, people who violently attacked the Jewish community have blamed their stance on Trump's being so pro-Israel.

On the other hand, there are those who call him an anti-Semite. And the latter label is even more incomprehensible because Trump has accomplished more for the Jewish people than any other president in US history. He has a consistent record of supporting Israel and the Jews in America; his daughter, son-in-law, and grandchildren are Jewish; he signed an executive order requiring federal agencies dealing with allegations of anti-Semitism on campuses to consider the complaints in light of the working definition of anti-Semitism. Yet he is still called an anti-Semite.

And the more Trump publicly supports the Jewish state and Christians who believe in the Bible, the more he is attacked with these nonsensical hate-filled accusations. Rather than attack his policies and his record, they attack him personally, manifesting what has been labeled "Trump Derangement Syndrome." What the haters are saying and why they attack Trump simply don't match the facts. But, from a biblical perspective, the reason they're going after President Trump in an intense and personal manner is because he's made his position clear: he's going to defend the Jews and Bible-believing Christians and support the Jewish state.

We find ourselves in the middle of what is referred to as "a clash of civilizations" between those who believe in the Bible (Jews and Christians) and those who actively deny the Bible (largely atheists and Islamists). This tension was recognized decades ago but is only now being expressed unchecked. Unlike the anti-Semites, Bible-believing Christians are not threatened by Judaism. They believe that they are grafted into this exciting chapter in history of Jewish return to the land of Israel. They see the people of Israel as the roots and themselves as a branch. They view the events in the land as a way to boost their own faith, and so openly express their support.

CHAPTER 6

The Fight against the God of Israel

The Jewish people represent the presence of God in this world; the covenant with Abraham, Isaac, and Jacob; and the promises made throughout scripture. One reaction to this awareness is humility and support, as Bible-believing Christians have recently expressed. Because they accept the Hebrew Bible and can see the prophecies coming true in the land of Israel, they choose to stand alongside Israel and the Jewish people.

Another response is an active rejection – fighting against the Jews, their country, God, and all they represent. In this chapter, we will further explain why certain groups are coming out so strongly against Israel. Their animosity stems from the rejection of God, Israel, and the Bible. And the more they see the fulfillment of prophecies in the land of Israel, the more they feel threatened. In response, they promote antagonism toward Israel.

The Only Free Democracy in the Middle East

Historically, many Americans have felt a connection to Israel, an allegiance motivated by common moral, political, and religious beliefs. They have also felt sympathy for this small country (nine million inhabitants in a country the size of New Jersey) surrounded by hostile enemies with hundreds of millions of inhabitants, whose leaders and citizens call for Israel's destruction and constantly attempt to infiltrate Israel and murder innocent civilians.

More notably, these Americans feel a kinship with the only place in the Middle East that shares their values – the only country that is democratic and industrious; respects and protects civil rights; provides freedom of worship to all religions; provides equality under the law to women and minorities; and that promotes and excels at education, arts, and science. They also appreciate that Israel is the only country in the Middle East where the Christian population is secure and growing. When such Americans look at Israel's enemies, they recognize them as opponents of the values they cherish themselves.

For these reasons, certain political alliances today are puzzling, and make no sense when examined strictly from an ideological point of view. The most baffling alliance is the cooperation between extreme liberals (including atheists and progressives) with Islamist extremists for the purpose of pushing an anti-Israel agenda.

At face value, the extreme left has nothing in common with radical Islam, which represents the antithesis of everything liberals espouse. And if one looks at the values promoted by these two groups, a liberal should be repulsed by the views of extreme Islam and the widespread violence and oppression in countries ruled by Islamic law. After all, modern-day liberalism is a movement for those who believe firmly in individual rights. Classical liberals tend to be part of a broader and richer tradition, including the appreciation of Western culture. One would expect anyone who stands for human rights to support the only place in the Middle East with a democracy and rights for all citizens. Nevertheless, we see an incredible effort to join forces with Islamist anti-Semites in what can only be described as an unholy alliance.

One place where these two groups converge energetically is on university campuses in Western countries. There, one can encounter some of the most egregious anti-Israel events and statements on the planet. Some universities permit the promotion of the false narrative of apartheid in Israel, allowing students to organize events filled with anti-Israel propaganda such as Israeli Apartheid Week. During this week, students have "die-ins" (protests in which participants fake being dead), and they fabricate claims that Israel is murdering children and committing similar blood libels. They sing songs calling for the mass genocide of Jews in Israel, chanting "From the river to the sea, Palestine will be free."

What this slogan means is that *all* of Israel should be wiped out and become a Muslim country. They're not talking about small settlements like Judea and Samaria, or the Golan Heights. They're talking about Tel Aviv and Haifa and entire regions.

Now, if we compare Israel to other countries in the Middle East concerning all the principles that liberals uphold, the difference is night and day. Sharia law, the principles that form much of Islamic culture, is the most intrusive and restrictive legal system in the world, especially for women. Women are considered the property of their husband or father. Husbands can beat their wives with impunity – and according to Sharia law, they *should* beat their wives – if they get unruly. In many Islamic societies, women cannot show their face in public. They are denied a formal education and often forbidden from driving cars (perhaps the biggest success for women's rights in the last fifty years in the Islamic world is that Saudi Arabia now allows women to obtain driver's licenses). Women can't go to sporting events, and they cannot be public officials.

More than two hundred million women worldwide have had genital mutilation forced upon them; the practice is common in the Muslim world. Horrible "honor killings" carried out by family members may be the fate for a woman who has dated a man without permission of her father, or kissed a man other than her husband. Child brides as young as six years old are sold. But on university campuses, no one seems to care – that's not the issue being brought up. Instead, they focus on the so-called atrocities of Israel, the only free democracy in the Middle East.

Now, if we compare the Muslim world to Israel, not only are women treated equally to men, but women in Israel enjoy the freedoms of emancipation more than any place in the world. Women can show their face in public and be educated and drive cars, and they can even become prime minister of Israel, as Golda Meir was from 1969 to 1974. Dalia Itzik was the only female Speaker of the Parliament in the entire Middle East when presiding over the Israeli Knesset (she was also acting president of Israel in 2007). The former governor of the Central Bank of Israel, Karnit Flug, was the first woman to hold this position in the Middle East. The chief justice of the Supreme Court of Israel is Esther Hayut. In fact, women are represented in Israeli government and professional communities more than women in other Western countries. The number of women with university degrees in Israel is greater than the number of men holding such degrees. Israel is one of the few countries with a mandatory draft for women, and women and men fight side by side in the military, participating in some of the toughest combat courses together.

Even with minimal research, it is easy to recognize that Israel is far above the cut when it comes to women's rights in every area of life. And when there's a situation in which one side is so in favor of equality and the other side is so egregiously opposed to women's rights – abiding by Sharia law, which seeks to regulate not only public behavior but private behavior and beliefs – you'd think that people on university campuses in America or in the media, which professes to care about individual rights and freedoms, would support the only place in the Middle East where these values are present.

Instead, it is common for student organizations at universities to demonize Israel as an imperialist power, even though more than half of Israel's population consists of Jews from the Middle East and North Africa, with a 20 percent Arab minority. They ignore the long list of horrific human rights violations throughout the Muslim world. These liberal organizations eagerly work with Muslims – although their views are diametrically opposed – with the common goal of promoting hatred for Israel and the Jewish people. Practically, it doesn't make sense.

Another example of the stark distinction between Israel and the rest of the Middle East is freedom of religion. In the Muslim world, other religions have no rights to worship or practice. One cannot be an atheist or Christian openly in that society – denying Allah or any part of the Koran is punishable by death. If someone takes a Bible into Saudi Arabia, for example, it's an incredibly dangerous risk, holding a stiffer penalty than bringing a kilo of heroin into America. People are subject to arrest and steep penalties for merely displaying a Bible in many Arab countries, and importing or distributing them can be even more dangerous.[8]

Israel, in contrast, has complete freedom of religion. You can walk around with a Tanach or a King James Bible or the Koran anywhere in Israel, including in the parliament or the main squares outside. You can conduct Bible studies or prayer services anywhere in Israel.

Ironically, the only place in Israel where not everyone can pray freely is the Temple Mount, controlled by the Islamic Waqf. The Temple Mount is the holiest site in Judaism and arguably the holiest site in Christianity as well. Despite the Temple Mount never being mentioned in the Koran, the Waqf forbids Jews and Christians from praying there and highly restricts visitation by non-Muslims. As a result, the only place in Israel without freedom of religion is the one place that is under Islamic control.

Yet instead of celebrating the fact that people in Israel have religious freedom, the organizations on university campuses don't mention a word about it, nor do they condemn the Arab leadership that denies those freedoms. Rather, they are consumed with condemning Israel.

Freedom of speech and of the press is another fundamental liberty protected in Israel and denied in the rest of the Middle East. The late Bernard Lewis, a leading expert in Islam, spoke at an event in Jerusalem and related that while he was in Jordan having dinner at an imam's house and watching Israeli TV, a Palestinian boy appeared on the screen wearing a cast on his arm. The boy claimed that Israeli soldiers had beaten him and broken his arm. He then vowed to fight against the Israeli police to get revenge for what they had done.

The imam looked at Lewis and remarked, "I would let the king of Jordan break both my arms and both my legs if only I could talk about it on TV. You see, in any of the countries around Israel, you're forbidden to talk to the media – you can't just say what you think about the government. And if you do, you can be immediately arrested and hanged for treason."

In Iran in late 2019, as many as fifteen hundred people were killed for simply protesting the government.

Not only does Israel have freedom of speech, it has some of the most liberal freedom-of-speech laws in the world. One can go on TV and speak against the Israeli government without any fear of retribution. Even in the Israeli parliament, about 15 percent of the Knesset is Muslim, and some have even called for the destruction of the State of Israel from the Knesset plenum by supporting the Palestinian National Authority's violent uprising – and they faced no repercussions. In many places, an elected official speaking in such a savage manner about the country that elected him would be tried for treason. But no one in Israel objects to such comments, as the country considers it as a form of complete freedom of speech.

Yet many professors and students on American university campuses verbally attack the only place in the Middle East that allows this freedom of speech and media, while supporting dictatorial governments that deny these freedoms.

Along with complete freedom of speech, Israel is the only place in the Middle East where leadership is elected through fair elections rather than imposed on the citizens. The Muslim minority population (nearly 18 percent) in Israel can vote for whomever they want to represent them. Sometimes their vote is for traditional Jewish parties, sometimes for left-wing parties, and other times Islamic parties. Israel has a representative parliament, in which approximately 15 percent is Muslim. There are Druze, a small Middle Eastern religious group, as members of Knesset. There are also Christian members of Knesset. It all depends on the voters.

In fact, Israel's democracy is sometimes viewed as being too liberal because of how often the country has elections.

Nevertheless, its citizens are proud of that fact, because they are the only democracy in the Middle East that conducts real elections. In other countries in the region, people are forced to vote for one candidate, and therefore, candidates often win elections by 97 or 99 percent.

And still, instead of celebrating the only place in the Middle East with a true democracy, many liberals spew hatred for Zionists while embracing radical terrorist organizations and oppressive codes of law.

The BDS movement, designed to hurt the Israeli economy, was started by notorious terrorist Omar Barghouti and is run largely by one of the most ruthless terrorist organizations, Hamas. And even though the Zionists are, in fact, the only free democratic country in the area, many of the liberals elsewhere side with the leaders who promote Sharia law, such as the Palestinian Authority and Hamas. While the PA wears suits and appears to blend in better with the Western world, one need only listen to what they preach publicly to their own people to understand that they are, in fact, no different than Hamas in their views.

Hamas held one election fourteen years ago and has forcefully ruled ever since. In Gaza, there are no rights for women under Hamas. There is no freedom of religion. The Hamas terrorist leadership often hijacks humanitarian shipments meant for civilians and reallocates the goods for terror. The same oppression is also common practice in the Palestinian Authority. Before the PA took over the birthplace of Jesus, the population of Bethlehem was almost 90 percent Christian, and the municipality was run entirely by Christians. But Christians have suffered incredible persecution under the Palestinian Authority. In just twenty-four years the number of Christians living in Bethlehem has dwindled to only 10 percent. Christians are routinely attacked, harassed, raped, murdered, and exiled.[9] The Palestinians, who are portrayed to the world as victims, are the persecutors.

If liberals were truly concerned with freedom and oppression, they would hold the Palestinian leaders accountable for the unfair and inhumane conditions they are forcing on the population. Instead, the Palestinian people are repeatedly oppressed and brainwashed by their leaders. Those who choose to enjoy the freedoms offered to them by the Israeli democracy are branded as traitors, and their families are ostracized and even targeted. Arab children are indoctrinated to commit violent acts of terror through cartoons and children's programs on PA television. These shows promote martyrdom and repeat poems and songs that demean Israel and call for violence. Yet few in the media or at universities talk about it.

Some sidestep the virulence of these anti-Israel protests and campaigns by saying that the animosity is all about justice and sympathy for the Palestinian people. But more Palestinians have been killed in the last five years in Syria than in the last one hundred years in Israel. Yet there are no rallies at the universities against Syria. Two million Muslims and thousands of Christians have been killed by Islamic regimes in the Middle East, but nobody is speaking out against those atrocities.

This "unholy alliance" is the coming together of Sharia law and American liberalism – and many of these liberals are Jewish. Bernie Sanders, for example, harshly criticizes Israel, throws around appalling accusations, and even gave a speech in which he said that some of the US aid to Israel should be given to Gaza. Walk into any of the hostile anti-Israel events on campuses and examine the crowd: almost half the room is white, extreme liberal, and atheists, while the other half are Muslims. From a practical and ideological point of view, such a scenario makes no sense. But from a biblical point of view, it makes perfect sense.

The Biblical Perspective

The unholy alliance between radical Islam and extreme liberals and atheists – even though they don't see eye to eye on any other issue – is built around their common disdain for Israel. But what lies behind their irrational hatred and obsession to condemn Israel? Either consciously or subconsciously, they perceive that the growth and success of this small nation demonstrates the presence of God in this world and fulfills biblical prophecies.

This idea that the God of Israel is real and the Bible is true poses a threat to everything that extreme liberalism and extreme Islam uphold. Islam believes that they came to replace both Judaism and Christianity, while atheists deny the existence of God and reject the Bible. Their internal dilemma remains. How can they continue to teach their children that the God of Israel is not real, and the Bible is a book of fables, as long as there is an Israel?

In response, both these groups work with all their might to bring down Israel in any way they can. They argue that Israel is a terrible country with evil people; the government is oppressive and unjust. They mislead the masses to believe that Israel a dangerous place, when, in fact, Jerusalem is statistically one of the safest capitals in the world. On university campuses, anti-Zionists try to intimidate any students who support Israel. In some cases, these students are forced to cancel trips to Israel or to resign from their leadership positions in student organizations. Jordyn Wright, a member of the Students' Society of McGill University's (SSMU) legislative council and board of directors in Montreal, was planning a trip to Israel. The trip, sponsored by Hillel Montreal, was scheduled to take place at the end of December 2019 and offered students the opportunity to meet with politicians, journalists, and residents to better understand the complexities and conflicts in the region. It also included visits to Palestinian areas. But when the SSMU Legislative Council learned of Wright's plans, they called for her resignation from student government and threatened to impeach her if she did not cancel her trip. Though the board later rejected the motion that had been passed days earlier, Wright had been publicly branded and humiliated.

One reason that these opponents of Israel are spreading lies, trying to scare people and keep them from visiting Israel, is that they don't want people to see for themselves what life in Israel is like. As soon as someone sets foot in Israel and looks around, the vibrancy of the country, the freedoms its people enjoy, and the false narrative they've been hearing from its enemies become immediately clear. The word "apartheid," for example, is thrown around flippantly. But anyone who walks around a shopping center or supermarket in Israel will notice Muslims and Jews working and living together. The liberals on Western campuses and in the media don't want people to see those things.

To clarify, the run-of-the-mill atheists or the classical liberal thinkers – most of whom may be less passionate about Israel – are not the ones spewing hatred. When asked about their critique of Israel, they may simply respond by saying something like, *We need to hold Israel to a higher standard because they're a Western, free democracy.* They are not consumed with hatred for Israel or the Jewish people. They can still recognize the virtues of Israel – the rights of women, the freedom of religion, the open practice of democracy – and admit that those important universal liberal values must be supported.

But here, I am referring to the extreme elements – the alliance between the highly active atheists and extreme Islamists – who are calling for the destruction of the State of Israel. And these same people are calling for the death of the Jews in Israel.

These extremists know that if they were to look at Israel without their bias and anti-Semitism, they would see prosperity and coexistence. They would see how a tiny country with no resources has become a light unto the world. They would see that people from all nations are coming to Jerusalem to praise God. They would see children playing in the streets of Jerusalem. And they know that if they allowed themselves to see all these things, they would have to admit that the Bible is true. So rather than seeing Israel for what it is, they go to great lengths to deny God's existence and the truth of the Bible, and to discredit and demonize Israel.

Out of a common desire, these liberals and atheists have joined with extreme Islamists to work against Israel, even though their liberal ideologies hold more in common with the democracy of Israel than with their fanatic cohorts. And while those who are threatened by the prophecies in Israel are uniting against Israel in a very powerful way, Christians around the world are joining with Jews in an unprecedented burst of activity, because they can acknowledge that the God of Israel is real, the Bible is true, and the prophecies are being fulfilled.

The Jewish people have been the most persecuted people throughout history. And those who have actively rejected God have come out against the Jews. We even find this in the Bible verse where Moses approaches Pharaoh in the famous scene and says: "Thus said the Lord, the God of Israel: 'Let My people go..."' And Pharaoh responds: "Who is the Lord, that I should hearken to His voice to let Israel go?" (Exodus 5:1–2).

Now, Pharaoh was familiar with the concept of God. The Egyptians worshipped all kinds of deities, and Pharaoh even considered himself a god. But he did not recognize the omnipresent, all-powerful God of Israel, and he scoffed at Moses and his God, which brought about ten plagues. Titus, whether he knew the Bible or not, thought that by conquering Jerusalem, he was defeating the God of Israel – which became a big priority for Rome. The Catholic Church and later offshoots historically believed that the covenant with the Jews had been voided. Yet the Jews in their country still represented a light unto the nations, through actions and abilities, a reminder that God is with his people – so mainline Christian churches tried to murder Jews throughout the ages, through crusades and pogroms, during the Spanish Inquisition, and ultimately the Holocaust.

Today, Israel as a nation has come into focus because it is known as the Jewish state. And as a result of God fulfilling his prophecies, this idea has become even more pronounced. That's why we're seeing many people who supposedly stand for the same human rights and values that Israel upholds being so anti-Israel instead. What begins with a subconscious motivation manifests in intellectual rationalization, so they use the Palestinians as justification to go after Israel. In truth, however, their animosity toward Israel has nothing to do with the Palestinian people. It's a way of rejecting the God of Israel.

Now, one may claim that liberals, atheists, and Islamists alike are unaware of the prophecies taking place in Israel. But most at least have a superficial understanding of the biblical covenant with the people of Israel, their connection to the land of Israel, and the promises that one day the Jewish people will return there.

If you take any secular, atheist Jew, for example, and go back a few generations, their great-great-grandfather was likely observant. The founding fathers of America were Christians who were familiar with Hebrew scriptures and prophecies. People have heard what the Bible-believing Christians are teaching, especially with the rapid global growth of the evangelical population (more than twice the world's population growth rate), aided by church leaders calling attention to the miracles in modern Israel. Likewise, Muslims have held conferences – before the concept of a Palestinian people was even created – discussing how people believe that God is fulfilling the biblical prophecies in the land of Israel. And they believed that if they could destroy the Jewish state, they could prove that the Bible is a lie.

While these people aren't viewing Israel through a biblical lens, they are aware of what God is doing in Israel. They know that the religious groups they most despise – evangelical Christians and Jews – are pointing out what's happening in Israel. And they believe that by defeating the State of Israel, they can prove once and for all that there's no God of Israel.

Passive versus Active Rejection

The rejection of the God of Israel and the Bible is ingrained in the extreme elements of the liberal movement, which is why they've become so anti-Israel and self-destructive. However, there are others, who have a more passive rejection of God and the Bible (they either don't believe or embrace it), who have no hesitation about standing with Israel. Many secular Jews, for example, love Israel. But those who pursue a more active rejection of the Bible and of God join the hate-filled campaign against Israel.

The general pattern has been that if you're actively trying to reject the God of Israel, you're bound to find ways to criticize the State of Israel and blindly embrace its enemies. While Christians and Muslims also believe in a Creator, the real source of anti-Semitism is the threat of Israel being the chosen people, the covenant God made with Abraham. It is this "everlasting covenant" (which we discussed in the first part, "The Alliance") that causes so much hatred.

For the same reason, Bible-believing Christians love the Jewish people and Israel: they believe that the covenant between God and Abraham is an everlasting covenant, and within that framework, God has a place for them too. They call this being "grafted in." They will, therefore, be included in the blessing of the Jewish people.

The same cause of hatred throughout the ages is manifesting again today against Israel. One difference, however, is that today we are not alone. There are Christians who recognize that the covenant is real and binding. They believe in the words of the Tanach. And because of that belief, they're standing with Israel, and they're being blessed for it.

CHAPTER 7

Radical Islam

One of the main groups of people who are against the Judeo-Christian alliance is radical Islamists. Why does Islam hate Israel and espouse anti-Israel rhetoric? What are the roots and causes of so much anti-Jewish sentiment?

The core problem between Israel and the Islamic world is *not*, as is often portrayed, a territorial dispute or a political problem – it stems from a religious conflict. The Arab nations see the mere existence of Israel as a threat to their ideology and, therefore, make every attempt to destroy it.

Since 2006, the majority of seats in the Palestinian Legislative Council have been occupied by Hamas. The Hamas Charter states that even Tel Aviv – Israel's most vibrant city, the economic and technological center of the country – is illegal and illegitimate, just like any outpost. In the Palestine media, Jaffa and Haifa and Jerusalem are all considered "occupied territories." It's clear that the true goal of Palestinian Arab nationalism is not based on the two-state solution but rather to conquer all of Israel.

For this reason, the "land for peace" approach has continually failed. It has only led to more death and destruction in Israel.

This is because the more concessions are made, the hungrier the Arab world gets for more land. From an outside perspective, you would think that giving up land would provide the opportunity to resolve the conflict, but the problems between the Palestinians and Israel – and the Islamic world and Israel – are complex. And to understand the true nature of the conflict, we must understand the culture in the Middle East going back before the State of Israel.

Traditional Jews view the return to Israel in the context of the fulfillment of the covenant mentioned numerous times throughout the Bible – the legacy of their forefathers who lived in the land of Israel. There were Jewish dynasties in Jerusalem, two Holy Temples, and a consistent presence in the land for thousands of years. After the expulsions, a small remnant of Jews always remained even while most were scattered throughout the world.

Yet the hope of returning to Israel remained alive in hearts of Jews across the globe throughout the centuries, on their lips in every Jewish prayer service, during festivals, and every wedding ceremony. Jews were often buried with a small jar of sand from Israel, the Holy Land. Even liberal modern Jews began moving to Israel after World War II – rather than to other places in the world – because they felt a deep connection to the land. They were ready to die in order to redeem their homeland and to once again live there in peace.

When we look at the other side, the Palestinian claim to the land, we must begin by asking the following questions: When was the beginning of the Palestinian nation? And when in history are the Palestinians first mentioned?

The natural starting point is in the historical texts such as the Koran in the seventh century. This primary source for Islam holds no mention of the Palestinian people or Jerusalem despite speaking of the Jews hundreds of times throughout the text. In fact, there is no mention of a Palestinian people or nation in any other Islamic text until the twentieth century.

From the birth of Islam until the twentieth century, the region we refer to as the Middle East was considered one vast country called, in Arabic, Sham. All the divisions that today appear on maps as Syria, Jordan, Israel, and Lebanon were nonexistent. The region consisted of a gigantic open space where people could travel from place to place. The Ottoman Empire offered migration and unrestricted movement of nomadic tribes – a common feature in Middle Eastern culture – throughout the land. During this time, Arab tribes of various lineages also settled in the land of Israel. But for the entire four-hundred-year period of Ottoman rule (1517–1918), there was never a political entity called Palestine or a people who identified themselves as belonging to the land of Israel – except for the Jews.

The borders we see on maps today are the result of the First World War, when the British and the French gained control of this region from the Ottomans and divided it into independent states that included Syria, Lebanon, and the Emirate of Transjordan. To appease the Islamic world, Transjordan was divided into what became the kingdom of Jordan and the British Mandate for Palestine – the land of Israel.

Only after the British set up the Mandate for Palestine did people begin referring to Jordanian people, Syrian people, Lebanese people, and Palestinian people. In fact, the term Palestine (which is how the British referred to the land) was often used by Jews who immigrated to the country – the Zionists also called themselves Palestinians – while the Arabs living in the land simply identified themselves as Arabs. That is why the original name of the *Jerusalem Post* newspaper was the *Palestine Post*.

In the media, Arab violence against Jews is often purported to be a reaction to the establishment of the State of Israel in 1948 or a result of Israel's victory in the Six-Day War of 1967 in which Israel captured lands in Judea and Samaria. But Arabs in the region were conducting organized attacks against Jewish communities even before the Mandate for Palestine was granted to Great Britain by the Allies at the San Remo Conference in April 1920.

Organized violence began in early 1920 when bands of local Arabs murdered Jews who had settled in the north and Muslim travelers murdered Jews in Jerusalem. In 1921, Arab rioters attacked Jews in Jaffa and its surrounding neighborhoods. The primary instigator behind these attacks was Mohammed Amin al-Husseini, who was at that point the grand mufti of Jerusalem and the highest-ranking Muslim political leader. A virulently anti-Semitic leader, he called for Arabs to "kill the Jews wherever you find them."

In 1929, al-Husseini and his followers fueled what was, in effect, a violent jihad. Brutal Arab assaults swept the land, including the Hebron massacre in which sixty-seven Jews were murdered. A mob carrying knives, axes, and iron bars slaughtered young students in the Hebron Yeshiva. Residents on their way home were lynched. Rabbi Ya'akov Slonim was the head of Hebron's Ashkenazi community. He had a good relationship with Arab neighbors. That all changed in an instant when an Arab mob broke in and slaughtered the rabbi, his family, and everyone gathered in the home, including women and children. The murder scene, recorded by Dutch-Canadian-American journalist Pierre van Paassen, was horrific.

In 1936, the Arab Higher Committee, led by Grand Mufti al-Husseini, launched another campaign of violence against the Jewish people. From 1936 to 1947, Arab opposition became more extreme and more violent. In 1937, the British Peel Commission proposed partitioning Palestine into Jewish and Arab areas. The Jews accepted the partition, but the Arabs rejected the proposal. They violently rioted against British rule. A three-year-long campaign of terrorism against Jews and British soldiers and officials led by al-Husseini became known as the Arab Revolt.

Al-Husseini also regularly broadcast propaganda over Nazi-controlled radio stations. In November 1941, he was officially received by Hitler. Both leaders firmly believed that Germany would win the war, and they met at the Reich Chancellery in Berlin to discuss what the Arabs could do to facilitate that victory.

According to the official German record of their meeting, al-Husseini explained to Hitler that the Arabs and Nazis had the same enemies: the Jews, the English, and Communists. And the Muslims under his control, he said, "were prepared to cooperate with Germany with all their hearts and stood ready to participate in the war, not only negatively by the commission of acts of sabotage and the instigation of revolutions, but also positively by the formation of an Arab Legion." Hitler then assured him that Germany would not intervene in Arab internal matters and stated that the only German "goal at that time would be the annihilation of Jews living in the Arab sphere under the protection of British power."

The mufti also wrote an anti-Semitic pamphlet for the thirteenth SS Handschar division, translated as *Islam and Judaism*, which was given to SS members. The pamphlet ended with a quotation from Islamic tradition: "The Day of Judgment will come when the Muslims will crush the Jews completely: And when every tree behind which a Jew hides will say: 'There is a Jew behind me, kill him!'"

Later, the Mufti continued his efforts to harm Jews by opposing all immigration of Jews into Palestine. During the war, he campaigned against the transfer of Jewish refugees to the country. He collaborated with the Germans in numerous operations throughout the Middle East and continually encouraged the Nazis to bomb Tel Aviv and Jerusalem to harm the Jews living there.

Revisionist History

Returning to the formation of the Palestinian nation and their claim to the land, a crucial change occurred when the region began to take shape as a result of colonialism. This period, when the land was divided, led to the creation of the countries we identify today. Jordanians, for example, are not mentioned before 1920. Neither are Syrians or Lebanese mentioned as a state.

During the 1920s and 1930s, Arab families immigrated to Israel (then known as Palestine) looking for work and found employment on some of the Jewish farms in newly settled villages. In 1948, during Israel's War of Independence against invading Arab armies, many of the Arabs living in Israel left as refugees. Many of those people simply returned to the countries from which they came – Syria, Lebanon, Jordan – but the Arab authorities there prevented them from going back to their previous villages. Instead, they were forced either to return to Israel in order to undermine the Jewish majority living there, or to live in refugee camps.

Thus began the Palestinian refugee crisis, orchestrated by the surrounding Arab states using their own people as a tool of propaganda. Arabs from different tribes and regions were (and are still) kept in refugee camps, the largest of which are located in the Arab states of Jordan, Syria, and Lebanon. Rather than accept their own people back into Arab society, the enemy states forced generations of families to suffer in refugee camps in order to cause international outcry against Israel.

Despite their origins, the Arab world demands the right for these refugees to return to Israel. And they hold special criteria for Palestinian refugees, unlike that of any other displaced people in the world. Only Palestinians and all of their descendants for every generation are considered refugees, while all other displaced people are counted only for the generation in which they were displaced. This has allowed the Arab world to inflate the Palestinian refugee problem and demand the right of return, not just for the thousands of Arabs who left Israel in 1948 but for millions of their descendants. The right of return states that as part of any future peace agreement with Israel, these millions of hostile Arabs must be allowed to live within the borders of the Jewish state.

In response to Zionism, the Arab world leaders bestowed Palestinian "peoplehood" on these unsuspecting Arabs and began to use the identity of the Palestinian nation as a political tool against Israel. To negate the right of the Jewish people to live in Israel, Palestinian leaders crafted a false narrative. Mahmoud Abbas, for example, asserted that the Palestinian people are an offshoot of the Canaanites who lived in the land before the Israelites settled there.

But when one examines what the Palestinians themselves say about their specific family origins, there is no connection to the Canaanite people. The Arabs who today refer to themselves as Palestinian have no language, religion, or culture that differentiates them from Arabs in Jordan, Syria, or other states. And many of their surnames testify to their true origins. If one looks through a phone book, for example, and checks the names of Arabs in Israel who identify as Palestinian, or those in Judea and Samaria, or in Gaza, many carry last names that are Egyptian, Syrian, and Lebanese.

Even fervent Palestinian nationalists, those who advocate terrorism against Israel, have occasionally admitted to many of the above-mentioned facts. Former Knesset member Azmi Bishara once stated publicly, "I don't think there is a Palestinian nation. I think this is a colonialist invention.... I think that until the end of the nineteenth century Palestine was the south of great Syria."[10] In March 2012, Fathi Hammad, Hamas minister of the interior and national security, traced the Palestinians' roots to Egypt, Saudi Arabia, and other Arab countries.[11]

On the one side of this conflict stands an ancient people, the Jews, who returned to their forefathers' land, a people who are mentioned not only in the Bible but also in the Koran. They are a nation tied to the land of Israel in the Bible, all their scriptures, and throughout the Talmud, along with almost every printed history book in the world. On the other side are a small group of Arabs defined as "Palestinians" only a few decades ago.

A Stark Contrast

Most of the Middle East today is a swamp of fire, tears, and blood, where citizens endure a low standard of living under an oppressive regime. In recent times, the Arab world has been involved in intense internal struggles and civil wars between Shia and Sunni and Islamists and moderates.

Israel, on the other hand, is the only democratic country in the region and has a highly developed free-market economy that ranks among the top countries in the world. The citizens in Israel enjoy extremely low unemployment levels, low inflation, and economic growth that is higher than the average of some of the world's richest economies. Living standards in Israel are better than in France, the UK, Italy, and Japan. Israel consistently ranks high among the world's economies in terms of its technological abilities, venture capital availability, and the quality of its research organizations.

In September 2010, Israel was unanimously voted into the Organisation for Economic Co-operation and Development (OECD), a forum in which countries committed to democracy and the market economy can compare policies and collaborate. The organization has praised Israel's scientific and technological progress and described it as having "produced outstanding outcomes on a world scale."[12]

The nation's economy is dynamic and competitive, aided by strong protection of property rights and openness to global trade. In per capita terms, Israel ranks number one in the availability of scientists and engineers, number of start-ups, and venture capital investments.[13] Its high-tech sector is competitive with Silicon Valley. Intel has been doing R&D in Israel since 1974,[14] joined by Microsoft in 1991[15] and Apple in 2012.[16] Other multinational high-tech corporations also choose Israel for R&D, including IBM, Google, HP, Cisco Systems, Facebook, and Motorola.[17]

As a result of its competitiveness and advanced technological capital, the Israeli economy is also relatively durable in the face of crises. The Bank of Israel has managed to avoid inflation even while the country has achieved impressive economic growth. In the health care sector, the entire population is entitled to comprehensive coverage provided by four competing health plans.

Buying in to the media propaganda, people are given a false impression: they see Israel's economic success and hear news about "the start-up nation" with all its global contributions. But then the media often twists the narrative by suggesting that these benefits, freedoms, and opportunities are reserved for the Jewish population, at the expense of the nation's Arab citizens and other minorities. In fact, the Arabs in Israel have the same rights as all other citizens. Roughly 20 percent of Israel's nearly nine million citizens are Arabs, the majority of whom are Muslims. In addition to all the freedoms previously discussed – women's rights, freedom of religion, free speech – Israeli Arabs receive free health care and education through high school.

At the time of Israel's founding, only one Arab high school was operating; today, there are hundreds. Israel's top technological university has seen the size of its Arab student body triple over the last decade. From 2008 to 2018, the total of Israeli-Arab students in master's degree programs increased by 90 percent. High-tech firms are opening offices and plants in Arab towns. In Nazareth, the largest Arab city in Israel's Northern District, close to a thousand high-tech employees work in companies such as Microsoft and Amdocs, 25 percent of whom are Arab women. Arabs in Israel also have equal voting rights, and Israel is one of the few places in the Middle East where Arab women can vote.

In contrast to Islamic societies around Israel that discriminate against other religions and women, there is not one privilege that a Jewish citizen receives in Israel that a Muslim citizen doesn't. The only legal difference between Jewish and Arab citizens of Israel is that the Arabs are not *obligated* to serve in the Israeli army, a law implemented to save Arab citizens from having fight against other Arabs.

In some cases, Israeli Arabs even have *more* opportunities due to affirmative action laws. The requirements for Arab student admissions in Israeli universities are lower than those required of Jews. Jewish students who aspire to go to medical school need to score twice as high on their MCATs as Arab students do. Though the Arab population is roughly 20 percent of the country's total, they occupy almost 50 percent of the dormitories at Hebrew University.

Clearly, the Israeli Muslim population has been the beneficiary of Israel's success. According to the UN World Happiness Report 2019, Israelis are some of the happiest people in the world. Israel's overall level of happiness has risen over the past decade.

Islam in America

Many Muslims came to America for a better life, searching for freedoms that they could never have in the Arab countries. Yet when one looks at the statements coming from Muslim communities in the Western world, it's clear that the advantages they currently enjoy in an open-minded liberal society have not changed their way of seeing the world.

There are plenty of anti-Israel protests in the name of human rights, rooting for an underdog against the bully regime. But how many demonstrations are there in Europe and America because of what happens in Syria, Libya, Yemen, and Iraq? If Israel defends itself against rockets being launched on innocent civilians – which no country would tolerate – suddenly, the streets are filled with political activists shouting "Free Palestine." When one million people are killed in Syria, the streets of Western countries are empty of protest. Why aren't there rallies clamoring that America needs to prevent Assad from gassing his people?

The activists' silence about the atrocities in the Muslim world, juxtaposed with their support of extreme terrorism against Israel, suggests that they are not really opposed to what's happening to their brothers and sisters throughout the Muslim world.

Looking at it pragmatically, Israeli Arabs, the Arab world in general, and especially Muslims in America should be standing with Israel. Of all Muslims in the Middle East, Arab Israelis have the highest standard of living. In the rest of the Middle East, the average citizen lives in squalor without individual rights and freedoms. They have no infrastructure. They're slaves to dictatorships. American Muslims, having left their countries in search of the same freedom and quality of life that people find in Israel, should surely embrace the only free democratic country in the Middle East. Yet they condemn Israel at every turn and support the aggression of Iran against Israel, the Palestinian Authority, and the international terrorist organizations of Hamas and Hezbollah. Why?

From a practical point of view, it does not make sense. But from a biblical point of view, it makes perfect sense. The reason many Muslims don't support Israel is that they see Israel through the eyes of the Koran, not the Bible. You can't teach your children that the Koran is true so long as a Jewish state exists in the heart of the Arab Middle East. Islam did not come into the world to live alongside Judaism and Christianity; it came to dominate other religions and to build itself on top of the ruins of Judaism and Christianity. Everything that was once Jewish and Christian became Muslim.

Therefore, many Muslims see a threat between Islam, which they call Din al-Haq, the true religion, and Din al-Batl, the false religion. According to Islam, Jews lost everything they once had in the world. They were thrown into exile by Allah and need to live as *dhimmis*, subordinate to Muslim rule, everywhere. But then, in 1948, the Jewish state was proclaimed and recognized by the world. In 1967, the Jews gained Jerusalem. If Jews continue to return, the prophecies continue to unfold, and the Holy Temple is built, Judaism – along with Christianity – will become a relevant religion once again, a thriving economy and free society right in the heart of the Arab world. And what then will become of Islam, which was to replace all religions?

Many Muslims simply cannot tolerate the existence of a Jewish state. It's a contradiction to the most basic principle of Islam. More than anything else, this perceived theological calamity lies at the core of their anti-Israel sentiment. And the more Israel establishes itself as a light unto the nations, a stable economy, and a Jewish nation that is here to stay, the more aggravated and fanatical they become. It's not a territorial problem, a national problem, or a political problem – it's a religious problem. From this stems all the violence, the anti-Israel descriptions and schemes in the media, the hostile demonstrations, and other forms of aggression toward Israel.

If you take the Bible and Koran out of the picture completely, everyone – especially the Arabs in America – would certainly praise a free democracy in the Middle East, which has produced incredible successes for its Muslim citizens, who can now live a better life than in any other Muslim country. Israel has all the freedoms of the Western countries, everything that you could ask for, with free medical care, education, and more. The only reason many Muslims reject Israel is that they still see it through the eyes of the Koran.

As Jews and Christians look at this picture through the eyes of the Bible, Muslims are looking through the eyes of the Koran. (Just as atheists and the extreme left are looking at it from a perspective of denying God, and mainline churches from the perspective of replacement theology.) And this is the sole reason that they oppose Israel.

Diverging Foreign Policy

Misdiagnosing the conflict in the Middle East has also led to a divergence in foreign policy. Over the past decade, two contrasting perspectives have steered American Middle East policy in general, and America's approach to Israel in particular. At the heart of the matter lies the different worldview policies of former president Barack Obama and President Donald Trump.

The Obama administration viewed the biggest challenge in the Middle East as the Israeli-Palestinian conflict. More specifically, Israel and the so-called occupation were viewed as responsible for the lack of peace in the region. And therefore, America needed to put more pressure on Israel to make concessions; this, the president felt, would solve the Palestinian-Israeli conflict and bring peace in the Middle East.

According to that doctrine, Israel was the biggest obstacle, while Iran provided the solution to the problem. Iran is a powerful nation that could bring order to the Middle East. The Obama administration, therefore, decided that the primary objective of US foreign policy was to reach an agreement with Iran. And former president Obama's burning desire to placate Iran came at the expense of Israel, the US's Sunni Arab allies, and the safety of millions across the world. The series of fierce uprisings, protests, and unrest called the Arab Spring that spread across the Middle East resulted from his attempt to bolster Iran and its influence in the region, to strengthen the Muslim Brotherhood in Egypt, Libya, Yemen, Bahrain, Syria, and Lebanon.

While Obama believed that by pacifying Iran and putting pressure on Israel he had found the solution to many of the problems in the Middle East, the Trump doctrine is exactly the opposite. President Trump sees Iran as the main problem in the Middle East. The fact that Iran is a powerful country trying to develop nuclear weapons and infiltrating weaker countries – Lebanon, Yemen, Egypt, Libya, and Bahrain and encroaching on Syria – is the main cause of instability and conflict in the region. And Israel, as the only free democratic state in the Middle East, is seen as the beacon. By standing with Israel and confronting Iran, Trump could help bring about a peaceful solution.

These two contradictory perspectives led to different strategies, which in turn created incredibly different outcomes. The former administration's emboldening of the Muslim Brotherhood in the Middle East and Iran led to the deaths of about two million Muslims, almost a million in Syria alone. It reached a point where, because of America's support of the Muslim Brotherhood over Egyptian president Hosni Mubarak, the Obama administration was considered persona non grata by Abdel Fattah el-Sisi, the new president of Egypt, when he took power. This was a shocking turn of events since Egypt was always America's top ally, after Israel, in the Middle East.

The Obama administration's policy also led to Hezbollah taking over the government of Lebanon. This internationally recognized terrorist group is now the leading faction in the government of Lebanon and in the Syrian civil war. It also led to the disastrous Iran deal, which shadily gifted $150 billion to Iran, the funding it needed to drive more terrorism all over the world and fund terrorism through its proxies in Gaza, Lebanon, and Yemen. It gave Iran the ability to develop nuclear weapons within ten years. Not only was Iran granted the ability to ramp up and rebuild its economy, to recover from sanctions, it will also be able to have nuclear weapons, nuclear facilities, and centrifuges.

The only good that came from the Obama administration's destructive doctrine is that the moderate Arab countries, such as Saudi Arabia and Jordan and Egypt, realized that they could no longer count on America – and so they started working with Israel. The relationship between Israel and these countries then grew because of the default position; they looked at Israel and said, *This is the only other major power in the Middle East. Therefore, we need to side with Israel.*

President Trump has a completely different perspective. His administration began once again to empower moderate Arab countries, while penalizing Iran by scrapping the Iranian deal, reimposing sanctions, and making statements that Iran will not be allowed to develop nuclear weapons. If one examines how many people were murdered in the Middle East during the last four years of the Obama administration and compares that to the first three years of the Trump administration, the estimated numbers are staggering. Trump's efforts to wipe out ISIS, which people said was almost impossible, have resulted in definitive gains against the terrorist group, which is no longer seen as a threat.[18] The previous administration had no policy for that. President Trump was able to push for the end of the Syrian civil war. He brought checks and balances to the Iranian aggression and built an alliance between the moderate countries and Israel. He was the first US president to fly a plane from Riyadh to Tel Aviv, signaling the beginning of a new chapter.

In early January 2020, Trump ordered the drone strike that killed Major General Qassem Soleimani, the head of Iran's Islamic Revolutionary Guard Corps, along with Abu Mahdi al-Muhandis, the commander of one of the Soleimani-controlled Shiite militias in Iraq. The IRGC runs Tehran's activities as the world's leading state sponsor of terrorism and was responsible for torturing and killing Iranians who protested the regime, plus thousands more in Iraq, Syria, Lebanon, and Yemen, and commanding attacks on Jews and Israelis. By killing Soleimani, President Trump made it clear that the previous administration's green light for Iranian aggression was off.

Not surprisingly, Trump's opponents deplored his courageous elimination of this vicious terrorist, some even showing compassion for the murderer. Ben Rhodes, the deputy national security adviser during the Obama administration who marketed the nuclear deal to the media, said Trump's move would lead to war. House Speaker Nancy Pelosi described the US strike against Soleimani as "disproportionate," as if it was a war crime to kill the terrorist who had just ordered his people to attack a US embassy.

Furthermore, President Trump announced that the United States would step up economic sanctions against Iran, with the goal to force the regime to give up its nuclear program and cease its terrorism and illegal missile production. In response, Representative Ilhan Omar – the very same politician who has fervently endorsed sanctions against Israel – tweeted: "This makes no sense. Sanctions are economic warfare." What makes no sense is the kind of double standards and biases that characterize anti-Semitism.

The main victims of radical Islam are Muslims, not Jews or Christians. People living under governments like Iran's are being tortured and killed. And yet there's been almost no backlash for it, because Muslims who moved to America for this better life and these freedoms don't see it through a biblical eye. They are more offended by a president upholding Judeo-Christian values than by the fact that Muslims are murdering Muslims.

Despite the notable progress in the region, the Middle East mostly paints President Trump as anti-Muslim and former president Obama as pro-Muslim. And that's because, once again, they're looking through a political point of view rather than a biblical point of view.

Bible versus Koran

The origins of Islamic hatred toward Judaism, and the conflict we witness today between Israel and the Arab nations, are just more links in the long chain of hostilities that have existed since 610 CE.

The basic tenet of some interpretations of Islam – the whole raison d'être – is that this religion came to the world to replace Judaism and Christianity. Bashing Jews for not converting to Islam was one method. Therefore, in the Koran, one can find statements about how the Jews are the worst enemies of Allah, how the wrath of Allah rests upon them because they didn't embrace Islam, and that they were turned into apes and swine.

When he emigrated to Medina, Mohammed became the ruler of the city. After a year and a half of attempting to convert Jews to Islam, he slaughtered them all in one day. Another group of Jews was massacred in an oasis near Medina. These killings are described proudly in his *Seerah*, the traditional biographies of Muhammad, which portray the history of early Islam. Those seventh-century sentiments are still echoed in the discourse and many of the slogans in the Islamic world today.

When Islamic anti-Semitism met Western anti-Semitism, Nazi ideas infiltrated the Islamic sphere. In the 1930s, Arab nationalists portrayed Jews as cockroaches. They copied images from *Der Stürmer*, a weekly German newspaper that was part of Nazi propaganda. Furthermore, *Mein Kampf* was translated and Arabized in Iraq: whenever the word "Aryan" appeared, they inserted "Arab" and adapted the book's ideas to relate to Jews and Christians, who do not fit the vision of how the Iraqi nation should look.

Over the years, followers of Islam continued to promote the idea that it was the true religion of truth while Judaism and Christianity were false faiths. This superiority to other religions is taught in schools, preached in mosques, and recycled in the Arab media. The establishment of the Zionist organization and the State of Israel added fuel to the fiery hatred.

The teachings of Islam claim that Judaism and Christianity lost their validity, their role in history, and all the assets they once had. Yet at the same time, Jews are coming back to their land, and in 1948 they established a state, which is recognized by the world. But according to Islam, Jews must be subjugated to Islam as *dhimmi*, a lower class of non-Muslims, and live under Islamic rule – they have no right to be sovereign on any land.

Making matters worse, the Jewish people gained control over Jerusalem in 1967. *What then will be the next step? Will they build a temple and bring Judaism back to life? And if this happens, what would that mean for Islam?* Before any dispute relating to territory, national rights, political rights, or human rights, the existence of Israel and the right of the Jewish people to live there is foremost a *theological* threat to Islam. They have no explanation for Jews coming back to the land and all the miracles and prophecies that have unfolded there.

The Islamic point of view stands in contrast to the biblical perspective; they're seeing this situation differently – with an ongoing disdain for Israel and America – because they're looking at it through the Koran, whereas Jews and Christians view the situation through a biblical lens. Since both the Jews and the Christians accept the Hebrew Bible and can testify to the prophecies, their religious point of view is in sync with the current events in Israel.

One of the reasons the Western world continues to misunderstand the conflict and has pressured Israel into making concessions that will ultimately endanger its well-being (and existence) is that they project their views and mindset, their scale of priorities, and their values onto a place that has a completely different culture. This belief that everyone wants the same thing as they do is the source of all failures to intervene in the Middle East. They misdiagnose the conflict because they don't have a proper understanding of the Islamic world, which operates according to a different set of rules and moral principles.

In America, for example, religion does not play an official role in political action and policy. Modern liberals often further try to marginalize everything that is connected to religion. In the Middle East, however, religion is the most prominent feature that plays a major role in anything relating to public life and determines government policies and actions. The religion of Islam dictates the rights of all inhabitants. Anyone who is not Muslim is an infidel, an outcast.

In Islam itself, the Sunni and Shia have been fighting over the succession of Mohammed for fourteen centuries – and continue to kill each other. If one observes the conflicts in the Arab world between the Sunnis and Shi'ites, Kurds and Arabs, the tribes of Libya and Yemen, and Iran and other Arab countries, it is evident that there is no clear domestic or foreign peace. So how can Israel be expected to make peace with an Arab world that cannot make peace within itself?

Every culture and religion possesses a different set of values and mindset, and it is a mistake to evaluate one culture using the measuring stick of another. In the Western world, where Judeo-Christian values pervade, there is great value placed on human life. Likewise, quality of life is measured by what someone has in *this* world – health, education, home, financial security, freedom, and opportunity. In Islam, human life is viewed differently. As in many religions, this world is only a corridor to the next world, an eternal afterlife, and paradise. For this reason, in many Islamic societies, martyrdom and violence are encouraged from an early age. And death is often viewed as more valuable than life, because of the glory it brings.

Even the concept of peace is viewed differently in Islamic culture, and therefore, by many of the key leaders. For example, as a result of how many Muslims interpret their religious teachings, there is an ingrained mentality that *prevents* peace with the infidel. According to Islam, seeking peace is a sign of weakness, a form of surrender that is condemned. In fact, the only treaties allowed with infidels are when they are deemed too powerful to defeat. In such a case, a temporary peace, or *hudna*, is then permitted. This also means that such agreements can be broken when the opportunity to attack presents itself. The peace treaty that Egypt signed with Israel in 1979, for example, was explicitly justified by the Al-Azhar, the supreme Islamic institution in Cairo, as a *temporary* peace. Yasser Arafat said the same about the Oslo agreements in 1993.

But the mainstream media never talks about these cultural differences. Instead, policymakers naively promote two-state solutions at cocktail parties and present theoretical political solutions as part of their campaigns. In reality, however, the conflict has nothing to do with borders or Jerusalem as a holy site – it's about the idea that no Jew should be living on Muslim land.

As such, the core conflict in the Middle East is rooted in how the leaders of the countries view the Bible. Without the Bible, for example, the founders of the modern state of Israel might have chosen Uganda (at one time considered by Theodor Herzl) or another remote place offering refuge to Jews after the war; they wouldn't care about having the Jewish state in the land of Israel. And if Arabs in the region didn't see the situation through the Koran, they'd be emulating the democracy and diversity of Israel in their own countries because they would value the things that Israel has – freedoms, economic growth, and equal opportunities.

CHAPTER 8

The Failure of Replacement Theology

Today, one of the most shocking groups choosing to stand against Israel is the mainline church. These churches, which include Presbyterians and Methodists in America, have called for people to pull their money out of Israel and declared that they intend to boycott Israel. Rather than embrace the only free democracy in the Middle East, they demonize the Jewish state and use church doctrine to defend their position.

One reason their position is so surprising is that these same churches are persecuted throughout Arab countries but enjoy complete religious freedom in Israel. Under Islamic rule, Christians are considered *dhimmi*, second-class citizens who are forced to submit and pay tribute. As the late Christian Lebanese president Bashir Gemayel once explained, "a Christian…is not a full citizen and cannot exercise political rights in any of the countries which were once conquered by Islam." In Egypt, Christians are often ostracized or insulted in public. And in some countries, only Muslim schools receive government funding.

Most places under Muslim rule are more violently oppressive for the native Christian communities. Damascus is only a two-hour drive from Jerusalem, but the Christians there are living in an entirely different world. Christians in Syria are given three options: they can convert to Islam, pay thirteen ounces of gold as protection money – a sum that most people there don't have – or they can be beheaded. Muslims in Syria have used the civil war as cover to massacre thousands of Christians there…all while the mainstream churches stay silent. There are no churches in Saudi Arabia. Though many of the foreign workers are Christians, they are forbidden to show any Christian symbols or Bibles or to worship publicly, and the penalties for defying these laws are severe.

Yet the mainline churches have decided not to vilify Syria or Saudi Arabia, but have focused their efforts on divesting from Israel. Rather than supporting the only place in the Middle East where Christian holy sites are protected and Christian worship is encouraged, these churches have chosen to align themselves with Islamic anti-Semites and stand against Israel.

Some endorse a movement called "Christ at the Checkpoint," which holds international conferences and lectures in Bethlehem. But these topics are not standard Biblical studies. Rather, in line with the mission of the organization, they focus on maligning Israel while portraying the Palestinians as helpless victims. During these presentations, they reiterate the lie that Israel is to blame for Palestinian terror. They have even gone so far as to reinvent the theological view of Jesus and have rewritten important biblical facts such as his religion and the location of important events in his life. Participants in this conference claim that Jesus was the first Palestinian martyr. The fact that Jesus was born Jewish and lived as a Jew in the city of Bethlehem – a city with a Hebrew name, which was part of the kingdom of Judea, seven hundred years before the creation of Islam – is something that most Christians know and accept. Yet these churches insist on

calling Bethlehem "occupied territory." According to their imagi-
nary scenario, if Jesus were alive today, he would be considered a
foreign settler living on occupied soil.

They also distort the facts by claiming that Christians are being
persecuted by Israelis. In fact, the situation is exactly the opposite. Israel is the only country today in the Middle East where the
Christian population continues to grow each year because Israel
shares the same values and freedoms as the Western world. In
contrast, towns under Palestinian control present a much more
troubling picture for Christians. In just twenty-five years since
the PA took over Bethlehem, the Christian population in the
birthplace of Jesus has dropped from 80 percent to less than 10
percent. The few brave Christians that remain in Bethlehem suffer constant harassment from the Muslim majority there.

The First Baptist Church in Bethlehem has been fire-bombed
and vandalized more than fourteen times by Islamists. Its pastor,
Naim Khoury, has been shot three times and left for dead because
of his support for Israel and defense of Zionism based on the
Bible. He and his followers live under constant threat.

In 2002, the Church of the Nativity in Bethlehem was taken
over by terrorists so they could shoot at Israeli soldiers, who
refrained from returning fire out of deference for the church.
Worshippers – nuns, monks, and priests – were kept in the
church as hostages by Palestinians, who ripped gold off the wall,
stole property, urinated on prayer books, and defiled the church.

Bethlehem is just one example. Unfortunately, there is ram-
pant persecution of Christians by Muslims in other Arab cities as
well. In September 2005, hundreds of armed Palestinian Muslims
crying "Allahu Akbar" attacked the Christian city of Taibe in Judea
and Samaria. For hours, the mob terrorized the community, setting fire to sixteen homes and businesses, looting, and destroying

a statue of the Virgin Mary. Christian graves have been uprooted in the Gaza Strip.

Christians are fleeing cities controlled by the Palestinian Authority for the same reason that Christians suffer in all the other Middle Eastern countries: religious persecution. In fact, Palestinian Christians have suffered as *dhimmis* and been the victims of violent attacks by Muslims long before the creation of the State of Israel in 1948.

The mainline church's response to Arab violence against Christians in Israel, however, is deafening silence. What's ironic about this is that part of the self-proclaimed manifesto of Christ at the Checkpoint is that "all forms of violence must be refuted unequivocally." Yet instead of acknowledging the persecution by Muslims and defending the well-being of Christians in the Middle East, these Christians focus their energy on demonizing Israel, the only country in the Middle East where Christians are *not* being persecuted for their religious beliefs.

The Palestinian Authority – whose official religion is Islam ruled by Sharia law – has no law protecting religious freedom. In 2000, in a sermon broadcast live on official Palestinian Authority television from a Gaza mosque, Dr. Ahmad Abu Halabiya declared that "Allah the almighty has called upon us not to ally with the Jews or the Christians, not to like them, not to become their partners, not to support them, and not to sign agreements with them."[19] The Palestinian legal and judicial system provides no safeguard for Christian landowners and enforces discrimination in education, cultural, and taxation policies.

In contrast, Israel offers Christians property rights, freedom of movement, clergy visas, and extensive real estate ownership across Jerusalem. The Greek Orthodox Church, for example, claims to be the second-largest landowner in Israel, after the Israeli government. The Knesset, the *parliament* of Israel, sits on land owned by the Greek Orthodox Church, to whom Israel pays rent. Israel is not only being open to the Christian community; they're being generous and accommodating; other countries would likely have confiscated the property if they needed it for government use. In Jerusalem, a Christian can sit on any park bench and read the Bible and teach and bring groups to visit the country. Fifty-five percent of all tourists to Israel in 2019 have been Christian pilgrims.

If these same church leaders were to try to operate in Saudi Arabia, they would be arrested. Yet the mainline Christian leaders still call for their congregants to divest from Israel. This double standard and lack of media coverage for Muslim intimidation and violence against Christians in the Arab world is glaring.

In another example of mainline Christian churches standing against Israel, numerous countries that are supposed to be Christian in nature supported a 2016 vote in UNESCO denying the Jewish people's connection to the Temple Mount or to Jerusalem. The resolution even referred to the holiest site in Judaism by the Islamic name, Haram al-Sharif. This attempted distortion of history is blatant considering that the origin of the word Al-Quds or Beit Al Maqdes is simply an Arabic translation of the Hebrew Beit Hamikdash, meaning the Jewish Holy Temple – a proof from Arabic that the Temple was already present in Jerusalem. Even the one-time mufti of Jerusalem Haj Amin al-Husseini, who genuinely hated Jews, published a brief guide to attract more tourists there. Since the land was then under British control, he published his guide in English. In that booklet, he wrote explicitly that the Haram esh-Sharif (the Temple Mount) is, in fact, the place where King Solomon built the Jewish Temple.

The Arab exploitation of the UN system to hurt Israel is not uncommon or surprising – but why are Christian countries joining this kind of Palestinian activity? Furthermore, the resolution essentially negates both Jewish and *Christian* history in Jerusalem. Yet many mainline Christian nations such as Russia and South Africa still voted in favor of the resolution. Other countries abstained, which itself was remarkable. Italy, for example, is a Catholic nation, yet still abstained from a resolution that denies any Christian connection to Jerusalem. This campaign proved the lengths certain churches are willing to go against their own interests, effectively denying their own history and theology, just to harm Israel.

This enmity has reached such an extreme that the Vatican's representative in Israel recently stated that he's a Palestinian first and a Christian second. In other words, their leadership has decided to identify with the political cause before they identify themselves as Christians.

Looking at the situation from the point of view of Christianity, which has been so vilified by Palestinians and the twenty-two other countries in the region, it makes no sense why mainline churches would ever adopt such a position. While at first blush, it defies logic for mainline churches to stand against Israel, from a biblical point of view their actions make perfect sense. The reason they are standing so strongly against Israelis is not that they truly believe Israel is wrong. After all, it's obvious to everyone that Christians are being massacred all over the Middle East while being granted complete freedom in Israel. Rather, mainline churches have chosen this path for the same underlying reason as anti-Semitism through the ages – the existence of Israel threatens their belief system.

Replacement theology has long championed the idea that the covenant with the Jews ended and was replaced with Christianity. Most adherents of mainline Christianity believe God's covenant is now solely with them. In previous generations, that doctrine sold. People were swayed to join in the campaign against Jews and embrace the teaching that they had replaced Israel as the chosen people – "the new Israel." And because that message was popular, it was acceptable to persecute and murder Jews around them. Today, in the context of the State of Israel, that message no longer makes sense. It's difficult to teach your community that God broke the covenant, or that Jerusalem was once a holy city until Rome took over as the religious center, while Jews have been returning to Israel and rebuilding Jerusalem in front of their eyes – exactly as the prophecies in the Hebrew Bible declared.

This change sheds light on another piece of the bigger picture involving the split within Christianity. In the past, almost all churches embraced some form of replacement theology. But a small remnant of Bible-believing Christians never accepted that doctrine. These Christians were unique in believing that the original covenant with Abraham is intact, "an everlasting covenant," as the Bible clearly states, and therefore the Jewish people are still the chosen people, the Torah given at Mount Sinai is an eternal covenant, and the prophecies will continue to be fulfilled. According to their belief system, Christianity can coexist with the Jewish faith. So long as Christians respect and embrace God's covenant with Abraham, Isaac, and Jacob and the land He has given their descendants to inherit, they too can share in the covenant, the blessings, and the destiny of the Jewish people in Israel.

Because of this love and loyalty to the Jewish people, the number of Bible-believing Christians has dramatically increased in recent years. As Israel developed into a vibrant nation, they were able to proclaim, *Look! All along, we were right – and the proof is Israel.* Pointing to the fulfillment of scriptural prophecies, they have been able to move people away from the mainline streams to become Bible-believing Christians. The land of Israel, therefore, became a central theme to illustrate to the masses how God's covenant is everlasting.

They also argue that when God makes a covenant, he never breaks it. Whereas, if the Catholics, Methodists, and Presbyterians are correct, then what stops God from breaking His covenant with them and choosing other good people? But since God *never* breaks his covenant, there's no danger of that happening. As a result of these explanations and calling attention to the Jewish people in Israel, the Bible-believing movement has been spreading like wildfire since 1948. That's also the reason why, in places from the Philippines to Africa, so many people have proudly declared their support for Israel.

In light of the events over the past seventy years, and the wave of support by Bible-believing Christians, many people began to reexamine the basis of the church doctrine on replacement theology, feeling that they had been misled for years. The impact of the challenge to replacement theology can be seen across Europe and Russia, where mainline churches are declining while Bible-believing Christianity is thriving. Mainline churches throughout Europe are empty while evangelical churches are bursting at the seams. This phenomenon has also spread throughout Africa, where one in two citizens is a Bible-believing Christian. Today Bible-believing Christianity is the fastest-growing religion in the world.

One great example of this phenomenon is Brazil. In 1948, the population of Brazil was almost entirely Catholic; today it's 35 percent Bible-believing Christian. And if you ask why they are

Bible-believing Christians even though their parents or grandparents were Catholic, most will reply that they no longer believe in a religion that claims to have *replaced* Israel. Rather, they feel that the biblical covenant with the Jewish people remains and that Christians have been grafted into this covenant.

A personal example that demonstrates the widespread embrace of Bible-believing Christianity took place in Papua New Guinea, on one of my tours to speak to different communities worldwide. The arranged lecture was to a group of painted tribesmen in the bush who didn't know a word of English, so I needed a translator. As soon as I mentioned the word "Jerusalem," the crowd started clapping and cheering – because they had all changed their indigenous beliefs to become Christians after hearing about the prophecies unfolding in Israel. The missionaries had used Israel to support their religious beliefs, even to people living in the wilderness of New Guinea completely cut off from the rest of the world.

There have been varying reactions to the rapid expansion of Bible-believing Christianity and the subsequent shrinkage of the mainline churches. Several mainline churches have admitted to their long history of anti-Semitism and have moved to repair their past mistakes. The Church of England, for example, in 2019 released a report that took three years to produce in which it admitted that centuries of Christian anti-Semitism facilitated the Holocaust. It also cautioned that "some of the approaches and language used by pro-Palestinian advocates are indeed reminiscent of what could be called traditional antisemitism."

Other churches, realizing that they no longer have a solid case for replacement theology in the face of Israel's reestablishment and the prophecies being fulfilled, are adapting to the current by incorporating certain Bible-believing ideas into their theology and becoming more pro-Israel. Pope Francis I, for example, echoed an evangelical perspective when he stated in 2013 that Jews are "our big brothers," the roots from which Christianity sprouted.

But many of the mainline churches have responded by sticking to their guns and taking an antagonistic approach to Israel. Threatened by the success and unfolding of prophecies, along with the massive wave of support flowing from Bible-believing Christians – all of which contradict their outlook – they seem to lose moral clarity and lash out against the only country in the Middle East that grants them full and protected rights with impunity.

They try, at all costs, to disprove the fulfillment of prophecies by discrediting Israel, and to deny the historical connection of the Jews to their land – even if in doing so, they remove their own religious ties to Bethlehem and Jerusalem. It's the modern face of ancient anti-Semitism trying to put down the Jews, this time driven by a fear that their own theology is wrong and that they're losing members.

What we are witnessing around the world is a split within Christianity wherein Bible-believing Christians are standing with Israel while mainline churches are standing against it. And as Bible-believing Christians develop more of a kinship with Israel because of their belief system, we can, unfortunately, expect some mainline churches to further focus their efforts to divest from and vilify the Jewish state. And this is why we are witnessing a movement of anti-Israel sentiment from extreme liberals, Islamists, and certain mainline churches. The alliance is not based on any positive connection, shared worldview, or uplifting message but on the strength of their common disdain for Israel.

PART 3
THE END GAME

CHAPTER 9

The Spiritual Battle for Jerusalem

While Bible-believing Jews and Christians are standing together, the people on the other side, who reject the God of Israel and the Bible, are banding together for the purpose of fighting a public war against the State of Israel. This conflict reaches a peak regarding the subject of Jerusalem.

The status of Jerusalem has increased tension on both sides, with politicians and the media adding fuel to the fire. To appreciate what lies behind the intense focus on such a tiny place in the world – and to uncover the motivation of both sides – it is important to first examine the historical and religious connection to Jerusalem.

What does Jerusalem mean to Jews and Christians? From a Jewish perspective, any discussion about Israel's holy sites begins with Jerusalem, which is considered the holiest city in the world and the eternal capital of Israel. For more than three thousand years, Jerusalem has played a central role in Jewish life – culturally, politically, and spiritually.

Not only is Jerusalem the site where the two Holy Temples stood, but Jewish scholars also relate that the Temple Mount was the very spot where Abraham bound his son Isaac. The name is first indicated in these biblical passages. After Abraham was instructed by an angel of God not to sacrifice his son, the verse relates that "Abraham named that place 'God will see,' as it is said to this day: 'On the mountain where the Lord will be seen'" (Genesis 22:14). The Hebrew word for "will see" is *yireh*.

Earlier in the Bible, after rescuing his relative Lot, Abraham was greeted by a man named Malchi-Tzedek, the king of Shalem, who welcomed him with bread and wine. The place Shalem, according to tradition, was the same site that Abraham would eventually rename Yireh. These two titles, Yireh and Shalem, taken together became known as Yerushalayim.

This combined title is explicitly stated in the book of Joshua (10:1), the sixth book of the Hebrew Bible, written more than twenty-five hundred years ago, and mentioned throughout scripture more than a thousand times. Also referred to as Zion (Tzion in Hebrew), Jerusalem is the spiritual center of the world and is the place where the Divine Presence of God, known as the Shechinah, made its final home.

The sanctuary constructed by Moses was already described in the book of Exodus: "And let them make Me a sanctuary, that I may dwell among them" (Exodus 25:8). This traveling sanctuary or tabernacle was, however, only temporary, as the Bible states: "For you have not yet come to [the resting place] and to the inheritance, which the Lord your God has given you" (Deuteronomy 12:9). That inheritance is Jerusalem.

Even though the Hebrew Bible spoke of the role that Jerusalem would come to play, it took many long years before those prophecies were fulfilled. After the Jews entered the land of Israel, they erected the sanctuary in Gilgal during the fourteen years in which they conquered and divided the land. From there, they came to

Shiloh, built a house of stone and spread the curtains of the sanctuary over it. They did not build a roof on it, or complete it, because the true house of God was meant to be in Jerusalem.

The sanctuary of Shiloh stood for 369 years. It was moved and stolen several times throughout the dramatic stories recounted in the books of Judges, Samuel, and Chronicles. Ultimately the tabernacle was moved from Givon to its home in Jerusalem when King David purchased the area of the Temple Mount and declared Jerusalem as the eternal capital of the people of Israel.

In the book of Psalms, David writes that "the Lord loves the gates of Zion more than all the dwellings of Jacob" (87:2). Although King David prepared extensively for the building of God's home, it was his son Solomon who constructed the Holy Temple in 826 BCE. The design of the structure built by King Solomon is described explicitly in the book of Kings.

For 410 years the Temple stood, until its destruction by the Babylonians. Less than a decade later, after many exiled Jews returned from Babylon, construction on the second Holy Temple commenced during the time of Ezra. The Jewish people built the Second Temple according to the structure of Solomon, including certain aspects that are explicitly stated in Ezekiel. It stood for 420 years.

Both Holy Temples were built in exactly the same spot on Mount Moriah. Although the Old City of Jerusalem covers only around one square kilometer, it was home to tens of thousands of Jewish pilgrims who would stream to the Temple on the three festivals of Passover, Shavuot, and Sukkot (Feast of Tabernacles), as commanded in the Bible. But in the middle of the first century, after the Jewish population rebelled against the occupying Roman Empire, Titus conquered and destroyed much of Jerusalem. Although the Temple was almost completely razed by the Romans, a small remnant of the retaining wall was left standing, the Western Wall.

The Western Wall, or Kotel, in the Old City of Jerusalem became the symbol of everything we had lost. It remained at the forefront of the Jewish consciousness. For thousands of years, Jews dreamed of appearing before the old stone wall, even just once, to beseech God and beg Him to rebuild the Temple and return the Jewish people to Israel from exile. No matter what period in history, or where in the world Jews were living, the bond with Jerusalem remained a focal point that played out in every aspect of Jewish spiritual life – in thought, speech, and action.

The centerpiece of the traditional Jewish prayer service for thousands of years is an elaborate prayer wherein we beseech God for all our personal and communal needs, three times daily. It is called the Amidah. Walking into a synagogue, it is easy to tell when the congregation is reciting the Amidah. The entire congregation stands in unison, facing Jerusalem, as every person concentrates intently on the words of the prayer book. This pinnacle of the service and deepest heartfelt prayer is not interrupted by any announcements or accompanied by any singing.

Consisting of nineteen blessings (praising God, requests, expressing thanks to God), the Amidah has several passages that reference Jerusalem and future prophecies: "Return in mercy to Jerusalem Your city and dwell therein as You have promised; speedily establish therein the throne of David Your servant, and rebuild it, soon in our days, as an everlasting edifice. Blessed are You, Lord, Who rebuilds Jerusalem.... Restore the service to Your sanctuary.... May our eyes behold Your return to Zion in mercy. Blessed are You, Lord, Who restores His Divine Presence to Zion."

At Jewish weddings, the groom places a glass wrapped in cloth under his foot and smashes it into pieces after singing the verses from Psalms: "If I forget you, O Jerusalem, let my right hand forget her cunning. Let my tongue cleave to the roof of my mouth, if I do not remember you, if I do not place Jerusalem above my highest joy" (Psalms 137:5–6). This custom is intended to remind everyone present that even at the height of personal joy, we must remember the exile from Jerusalem and yearn to return there.

At the time of its destruction, the entire nation of Israel mourned this loss. All Jews, including those who lived far from Jerusalem, were agonizingly heartbroken by the exile from their holy city. Since then, on the ninth of Av, which is the Hebrew date that both Temples were destroyed, Jews fast and mourn. After two millennia, Jews still grieve the loss of the Temple in Jerusalem, but the Jewish people have never lost hope that it will one day be rebuilt and Jerusalem will be restored to its former glory.

There is a famous story in Jewish tradition about four great rabbis (Rabban Gamliel, Rabbi Elazar ben Azariah, Rabbi Joshua, and Rabbi Akiva) who traveled to Jerusalem after the destruction of the Temple by the Romans. When they reached the Temple Mount, they saw a fox emerging from the place where the Holy of Holies once stood. Three of the rabbis began to weep, but Rabbi Akiva began to laugh. The others, puzzled by his reaction, asked him how he could laugh while wild animals roamed the most sacred biblical site.

Rabbi Akiva then pointed to two scriptural prophecies – the first dealt with the destruction of Zion, which will be "plowed like a field," and the second prophecy provides a vision of the Jewish return to their homeland when men and women will once again sit in the squares of Jerusalem, grow old there, and the streets will be filled with children playing.

He then explained to his colleagues how these specific prophecies are inherently linked. And once Rabbi Akiva witnessed the fulfillment of the bitterness of the prophecy that led to exile, he was certain that Zechariah's prophecy of redemption would also happen in the fullest measure.

While the other rabbis had faith that future prophecies would come true, only Rabbi Akiva could detect a vision of future glory within the present ruins. He believed so much that the Temple would be rebuilt, he was able to momentarily celebrate even during the greatest tragedy. After his explanation, the rabbis replied to him: "Akiva, you have consoled us!"

More recently, the story is told about the French emperor Napoléon Bonaparte, who while traveling through a small Jewish town during the early 1800s entered a synagogue on the ninth day of Av, the day of mourning for the Temple. Inside, he noticed men and women sitting on small stools, weeping, holding candles while chanting verses from the Book of Lamentations and reading prophetic writings. Though the synagogue had an elegant chandelier, the room was dark and only a few candles were lit.

After the emperor inquired about the cause for their mourning, a French officer who knew about the Jewish anniversary explained to Napoléon that these solemn ceremonies were conducted for the destruction of their Holy Temple in Jerusalem. Napoléon expressed astonishment that he had heard nothing about this tragedy from his intelligence sources. When it was further clarified that this event took place close to eighteen hundred years earlier, Napoléon reportedly exclaimed, "A people who can still mourn for their Temple, and their homeland, after so many years, will one day merit to see it rebuilt."

The Jewish connection to Jerusalem is so pervading that it appears even when comforting those who have experienced a death in their own family. The traditional words of consolation expressed to mourners are "May the Almighty comfort you amongst the mourners of *Zion and Jerusalem*" (emphasis added). The final phrase conveys the idea that just as it gave strength and courage to the Jerusalemites to know that the entire people were feeling their pain, so too now, while an individual or family is mourning, they are reminded that the entire Jewish people share in their sorrow.

Looking to the future, Jews have always concluded their Passover Seder and Yom Kippur service by singing "Next year in Jerusalem! Next year in a rebuilt Jerusalem!"

Unfortunately, until recently, Jerusalem hasn't been easily accessible for Jews. When the crusaders ruled the land, for example, no Jew could safely reside there. Under the subsequent centuries of Muslim rule, admission was strictly limited. And no prayer services could be held there. After the War of Independence in 1948, a wall was erected that cut through the middle of the city, and Arab residents expelled all Jewish inhabitants from the Old City. Despite the terms of the agreement, Jews were still denied access to the Western Wall as well as their ancient cemeteries.

After the miraculous victories of the Six-Day War, the city of Jerusalem was reunited, and finally, Jews could worship at their holy sites in Jerusalem.

But the significance of this city for Jews consists not only of a rich history and deep religious connection – it's also the place where the final prophecies must be fulfilled. The main prophecies yet to occur are the rebuilding of the Temple in Jerusalem and the coming of the Messiah, at which time there will be an end to all suffering and true peace and harmony will prevail.

Christians, although they have a different view of the Messiah, also see Jerusalem as crucial to this prophecy. Both religions eagerly await this final stage when the Messiah will come – but that's not going to happen if the Jewish people give away Jerusalem.

For this reason, along with the above significance, the issue of Jerusalem is an issue that people who believe in the Bible have always kept close to their heart. The verse in Psalms states: "Pray for the peace of Jerusalem; may those who love you prosper. May there be peace within your walls, prosperity in your palaces" (Psalms 122:6–7). This is the only place in the Bible that God asks us to pray for something. The question remains: Why would the Creator of the universe need us to pray for Jerusalem? One explanation is that God wants us to remain focused on Jerusalem, so we don't lose Jerusalem as the capital of Israel.

As mentioned in chapter four, Christians began a movement in 2004 to establish a new holiday in the Christian calendar called the Day of Prayer for the Peace of Jerusalem. Today, millions of Christians around the world conduct prayer meetings for Jerusalem on the first Sunday of every October because they believe that they are obligated, according to scripture, to support and pray for the State of Israel.

These Christians recognize that their belief in the Bible connects them to the land and the people of Israel. And Jews throughout the world began joining them on this day to participate in praying for the peace of Jerusalem.

What Does Jerusalem Mean to Islam?

While the historical and religious connection of Jerusalem to Jews and Christians is clear, as well as the profound role of the city in fulfilling the remaining prophecies, the tie to Islam is questionable. Over three thousand years ago, before Mohammad received his visions, the Arab forefathers were wandering the desert, but Jews were worshipping God in Jerusalem. Jerusalem is mentioned 660 times in the Hebrew Bible (and the synonym "Zion" occurs

158 times), yet Jerusalem is *never* mentioned in the Koran. Even politically, Jerusalem was never, not even for a day, the capital of anything connected to the Arab or Islamic world.

The notion of Jerusalem as a holy city for Islam was created by a group of Muslims who controlled the Islamic world between 661 and 750 CE. After a rebellion that erupted in Mecca in the year 682 – fifty years after Muhammad died – they designated Jerusalem as an alternative place for pilgrimage (hajj) instead of the traditional city of Mecca. They did so by manipulating a story in the Koran that details one of Mohammad's dreams, known as the Night Journey. The story explains that he traveled to "the farthest mosque" on a flying horse. This mosque, called Al-Aqsa, was said to be located between two cities in the Arabian Peninsula. The scholars switched the site from the Arabian Peninsula to Jerusalem, therefore justifying their decision to divert the hajj from Mecca. It is important to note that Mohammad's vision occurred in 621 CE, and the Al-Aqsa Mosque in Jerusalem was not built until 705. By declaring Islamic sanctity to the place that was holy only to the Jews for thousands of years prior to the invention of Islam, Muslims embarked on a campaign to build over Jewish holy sites to conceal the truth of their deception.

The entire story about the sanctity of Jerusalem in Islam is based on a struggle within Islam that took place between the center of Damascus and the center of Mecca. Notably, the Shia, one of the two main branches of Islam, never agreed to this view of Jerusalem and regarded it as any other city on Earth. Even Sunni Muslims and scholars who lived in the Middle Ages acknowledged that this portrayal of Jerusalem as a holy place was disinformation and likewise viewed Jerusalem as a regular city, no different than any other place in the world.

Fast-forward to 1930, when the pamphlet published by the Supreme Muslim Council acknowledged the Temple Mount as the site of King Solomon's Temple – a matter "beyond dispute" and accepted as "universal belief." Furthermore, Jordanian maps until 1967 refer to the Temple Mount as Mount Moriah.

Today, however, a new narrative is disregarding all that the historical documents – including Biblical passages, Greek and Roman writings, and archaeological findings – have taught us. The story of Jerusalem that was once linked to Jews and Christian heritage is being recast as an exclusively Muslim one.

The Temple Mount suddenly became known as Al-Aqsa, with no further mention of Mount Moriah on any printed map. Revised pamphlets are now distributed by the Muslim Waqf – an Islamic trust that manages the current edifices surrounding the Temple Mount. They deny that the Temple ever stood atop the Temple Mount and reject any historic and religious connection of the Jewish people to the Western Wall. The existence of the Jewish Temple and the Jewish people in Jerusalem was erased from Islamic history. This also resulted in the negation of the Christian connection to Jerusalem. This Islamic attempt to reinvent history also aims to disprove the Bible.

But while the Muslims were scrambling to rewrite history, Israeli archaeologists were uncovering evidence that proved the Jewish and Christian connection to Jerusalem and the Temple Mount. In response, the Muslim leadership embarked on a campaign to destroy antiquities and archaeological evidence that would contradict their new account. The Muslim Waqf forbid Israeli archaeologists from conducting excavations on the Temple Mount. Then, in 1999 under the guise of renovations, the Waqf used bulldozers to dig up and dump more than nine thousand tons of earth and artifacts from where the Jewish Temple once stood.

Political opponents of Israel have followed suit by adopting a series of UN resolutions aiming to erase the Jewish and

Christian historical connection to Jerusalem. The recently adopted UNESCO resolution (discussed in chapter eight) denies the historical connection of Jews and Christians to Jerusalem – most notably to the Temple Mount and the Western Wall – as well as condemning ongoing archeological excavations in ancient Jerusalem whose discoveries regularly affirm such connections.

Among those people propagating this false narrative is the current chairman of the Palestinian Authority, Mahmoud Abbas, following in the footsteps of former chairman Yasser Arafat, along with other notable Palestinian academics, politicians, and religious leaders.

To confuse the issue, those against Israel are trying to turn the struggle over Jerusalem into a *political* issue – a territorial dispute. They portray the city of Jerusalem not as one united metropolis but as containing two distinct sections. Seen in this way, it is easier to push the proposed solution: give the Arabs "East Jerusalem," and let the Jews have "West Jerusalem" – then everyone will be happy, it's said.

But there is only *one* Jerusalem – and the focus on Jerusalem is essentially a biblical issue. What people refer to as *East* Jerusalem is the center of the holiest sites: Jerusalem's Old City, the Kotel, the Western Wall, and the Temple Mount. East Jerusalem is also the location of important Christian holy sites such as the Garden Tomb, the Cardo where Jesus walked through the Old City, and the location (the Temple Mount) where Jesus overturned the tables of the moneylenders. In fact, every site that is holy to Jews and Christians is in what the world calls East Jerusalem. Why? Did God say to King David, *Build in the east part of the city?* Of course not.

The truth is that until the early 1900s, everyone lived in Jerusalem's Old City; but as the population grew, they started building the suburbs to make room for the expanding population. When people today propose "dividing Jerusalem," what they're really asking Israel to do is to give away the heart and soul of the Jewish people, the Old City of Jerusalem. And for Jews and Christians, this move would be a critical mistake, because for the final prophecies to be fulfilled – the *complete* reestablishment of the nation of Israel within the land of Israel – Israel must have autonomy in Jerusalem.

It is paramount that the land of Jerusalem remains united, because this is a theological issue, not a national or political dispute. This also explains why an evangelical Christian living in Oklahoma or Australia is so concerned that Jerusalem remains whole. These Christians understand that if Jerusalem is divided and the Old City is lost, then the next prophecies will be further delayed.

The other side also understands this. Therefore, their relentless pursuit to divide and claim Jerusalem (more than any other part of Israel) for the Palestinians is not because Jerusalem is important to them but because they know the real connection between the Jewish people and this holy city.

Historical studies can easily determine that Jerusalem was Jewish long before Islam came on to the scene. There are even passages in the Koran confirming the Biblical connection of the Jewish people to the land of Israel, the building of Solomon's Temple in Jerusalem, and Jewish sovereignty there.[20] And the world should accept these facts. Logically, Jerusalem should be left to its rightful historical and religious owners. But the opposition to this is not just about Jerusalem. It stems from the need to prove that Islam has some validity. The Palestinians, in turn, understand that if they lose Jerusalem to Israel, they will be blamed by the Muslim world and suffer severe consequences – and so, this effort intensifies.

A similar pattern can be seen historically. Jerusalem's Old City is surrounded by ancient walls, which served as a fortress throughout its history. The existing walls were built by Sultan Suleiman in the middle of the sixteenth century, partly on the remains of the ancient walls. The walls contain eleven gates, and only seven of those gates are open for passage. One of the closed gates is called the Golden Gate, located below the Temple Mount. Jewish literature details that when the Messiah comes, he will enter Jerusalem through that gate. To prevent this from happening, the Muslims sealed the gate during Suleiman's rule in the 1500s.

The same attempt in a different form is taking place in our lifetime – to erase the legitimate connection of the Jews to Jerusalem and convince the world to divide the land. This especially concerns the opposing forces now that all the other prophecies are being fulfilled before their eyes. If the Jewish people lose even part of Jerusalem, it will represent a major victory for the opposition, which can then say, *Look, all those other successes in Israel were just a coincidence, not a sign of divine providence. After all, the Jews don't even have Jerusalem. They didn't return to their land completely. There will not be a rebuilt Jerusalem or a coming of the Messiah.*

Because of this underlying desire to disprove the prophecies, they're trying to not only divide Jerusalem for political purposes but to destabilize Jerusalem. Hence, the Waqf pamphlet denying that the Temple ever stood atop the Temple Mount, and the UNESCO resolution erasing the historical connection of Jews and Christians to Jerusalem and claiming that these sites are Muslim landmarks, along with condemning Israeli archaeological excavations whose discoveries regularly affirm the actual historical connections.

Unfortunately, much of the Western secular media has bought in to the fake Islamic claims to Jerusalem and joined in the fight against Israel. This has allowed the demonization of Israel to become widely accepted. In fact, the European Court of Justice has ruled that since it considers Jews to be occupiers of Jerusalem, all goods produced by Jews in what the ECJ calls "East Jerusalem" need to be labeled "made in occupied territory."

This desire to strip Jerusalem of its true heritage is also why the Obama administration initiated a building freeze in Jerusalem only for Jews. Arabs continued to build illegally and dangerously throughout the Holy City, unchecked. This policy allowed the Arabs to steal vital parts of Jerusalem to further their goal of planting facts on the ground. The European Union has also become involved by funding the illegal construction of Arab buildings with the intent to connect Ramallah to Bethlehem through Jerusalem. The outcome of this project would cut Jerusalem in half, effectively taking the Old City for the Arabs and creating obstacles that make it harder to view Jerusalem as a united city.

The good news is that Jews are most of the population living in "East Jerusalem" today. Because of this and the fact that now President Trump has allowed Israel to build its capital there, more communities are developing in that part of Jerusalem as the Jewish community there is pushing back by building homes. But at the same time, they remain aware that the other side is working fervently to undermine the idea that Jerusalem is the capital of Israel and that the Jewish people have claim to *all* of Jerusalem, and attempting to use political power such as financial sanctions, labeling laws, and the BDS movement to destabilize Jerusalem.

The Evidence of Archaeology

But even as international organizations have joined the Arabs in denying the Jewish connection to Jerusalem, Israeli archaeologists continue to unearth artifacts that prove the Jewish presence in the Holy City dating back thousands of years. We previously mentioned the Waqf's illegal destruction on the Temple Mount and their attempt to dump Jewish artifacts as garbage. What is less well known is how a team of faithful Jews took possession of the nine thousand tons of rubble dumped by the Waqf and have been painstakingly sifting it one bucket at a time.

Among the most exciting things happening in Israel today, especially for those who questioned the facts behind the biblical stories, are the recent archaeological discoveries at the foot of the southern wall of the Temple Mount. For nearly two thousand years, the Jerusalem of ancient times, referred to as the City of David, lay hidden until a British archaeologist, Charles Warren, who was involved in researching the Temple Mount beginning in the 1860s, uncovered rich relics from the first of two Jewish Temples – beginning a series of discoveries that continue until today.

The City of David is now the largest archaeological site in Jerusalem. The site attracts about five hundred thousand visitors a year and offers families guided tours through the excavations and a 3-D exhibition. Tourists are treated to an experience of ancient Jewish history as they walk through the places where Malchi-Tzedek blessed Abraham, where Jewish kings were anointed, and where Isaiah and Jeremiah prophesied to kings inside the palace area.

The ongoing archaeological finds, deep under the City of David, are exposing some of the most unique discoveries of our time. In 2015, excavations under the leadership of Dr. Eilat Mazar of the Hebrew University discovered the private seal of one of the more important figures in the Bible, King Hezekiah, who helped transform Jerusalem into an ancient metropolitan area during the eighth century BCE. The Bible describes him as a courageous ruler, someone who "trusted in the Lord, the God of Israel," and states that "there was none like him among all the kings of Judah, either before him or after him" (2 Kings 18:5).

The tiny clay seal, used for sealing official documents, clearly shows his royal signature with the title "King of Judah" and the precise artistic design that he chose for the seal – a sun disk signifying the power of God, as alluded to in Psalms 84, with wings alongside a universal symbol of life. It was most likely handled only by the king himself.

This is the first time that a seal impression of a Judean king has been found in an organized archaeological excavation, providing further historical evidence for the centralized Jewish government that once operated in the ancient city of Jerusalem.

Israeli archaeologists led by Mazar also discovered two clay bullae (seals) of royal officials in the City of David. These seals, from the sixth century BCE, inscribed with ancient Hebrew, bear the names of Jehucal son of Shelemiah and Gedaliah son of Pashhur. The names of these individuals correspond to King Zedekiah's ministers who unsuccessfully plotted to kill the prophet Jeremiah. Furthermore, these two names appear in the same verse in the book of Jeremiah: "And Shephatiah the son of Mattan, and Gedaliah the son of Pashhur, and Jehucal the son of Shelemiah, and Pashhur the son of Malchiah, heard the words that Jeremiah spoke unto all the people..." (Jeremiah 38:1).

The discovery of these twenty-six-hundred-year-old seal impressions marks the first time in the history of Israeli archeology that two clay bullae containing two Biblical names that appear in the very same verse in ancient scripture have been found in the same site.

Among the assemblage of other seals in the excavation was an artifact bringing another iconic biblical figure to life – the prophet Isaiah. King Hezekiah and this prophet are linked in numerous scriptural passages that mention the two individuals in the same sentence. When the Assyrians had conquered Judah's fortified cities, the Assyrian ruler Sennacherib and his army had conquered all the areas surrounding Judea and stood at the gates of Jerusalem, ready to attack. He then – while cursing God – asked Hezekiah to surrender. King Hezekiah and his nation were trapped in the fortified city. He prayed for deliverance and called in his spiritual advisor, the prophet Isaiah. Isaiah then delivered a strong message – "Do not be afraid!" That night, the Biblical narrative relates that an angel of God killed all the Assyrian troops.

In the recent excavation, a tiny clay piece was discovered near the seal of King Hezekiah, another seal impression, which may have belonged to the prophet Isaiah. Such a finding marks the first-ever archaeological evidence of the biblical prophet Isaiah.

Perhaps the most famous part of the City of David is Hezekiah's water tunnel, which served as a reservoir for the waters of the Gihon Spring, Jerusalem's main water source during the First Temple period, as referenced in the book of Nehemiah: "He also repaired the wall of the Pool of Shelah by the king's garden, even as far as the stairs that go down from the City of David" (Nehemiah 3:15).

During Temple times, hundreds of thousands of Jewish travelers would ascend to the Temple during the three festivals of Passover, Shavuot (Pentecost), and Sukkot (Tabernacles). But before going to the Temple, Jewish law requires one to purify oneself by immersing in a natural body of water, called a mikvah.

During the late Second Temple period, the Pool of Siloam – the size of two Olympic swimming pools – served as this ritual bath. And beneath this Herodian-style pool, archeologists found the original Pool of Siloam (the same as the Pool of Shelah previously mentioned) engineered by King Hezekiah.

These are just some of the many new discoveries, which include a rare etching of the menorah, one of the primary holy objects used in the Temple service and which later became the national emblem of the State of Israel.

> And you shall make a menorah of pure gold. The menorah shall be of hammered work, even its base, and its shaft; its cups, its knops, and its flowers, shall be of one piece with it. And there shall be six branches going out from its sides: three branches of the menorah out of the one side and three branches of the menorah out of the other side. (Exodus 25:31–32)

The third phase of Dr. Eilat Mazar's excavation has recently been completed in a spot that she believes to be the site of King David's palace.

As one reads the Bible, encountering the struggles, successes, and failures of mighty characters, people are sometimes led to believe these are just stories. In truth, the Bible taught about real people. The recent excavations are uncovering the actions of key biblical personalities of the past, while the biblical verses are helping to explain the findings – an interplay between archaeology and prophecy. Together they are providing us with a more complete picture of ancient Jerusalem.

Furthermore, the timing is no coincidence. If some of these items had been discovered a hundred years ago, few would have paid attention. Today, in the wake of all the attempts to deny the

Jewish people's connection to the land, God is providing proof – not only that Holy Temple stood on the Temple Mount but that King David and other kings had their capital city in Jerusalem. It's as if ancient Jerusalem is sharing her story with us for a reason.

A Pivotal Move

As part of their scheme, Arabs have asserted the fact that many countries have not yet moved their embassies to Jerusalem is proof that the world agrees that Jerusalem does not belong to Israel. Although as mentioned in chapter six, the true desire of the Arab nations is for *all* of Israel – "from the river to the sea" – they don't bring up Tel Aviv or Ber Sheva to the media because they know that the world will not jump on board. But when it comes to Jerusalem, unfortunately, much of the world bought in to their propaganda and allowed Jerusalem to become a focal point in the conflict, lending credence to the Arab claim on the city.

For this reason, Donald Trump's decision to move the embassy from Tel Aviv to Jerusalem and declare it the capital of Israel was probably the most significant event in our lifetime when it comes to Israel. For the first time, it was clear that the superpower in the world had declared that Jerusalem is the center of the Jewish faith.

There are those who claim that Trump's decision to move the embassy to Jerusalem was not a big deal – it doesn't really have significant repercussions. But in reality, people follow symbols. The end of communism was marked by the falling of the Berlin Wall. The statue of Saddam Hussein toppling in Iraq represented the end of the Iraqi war. And the United States embassy being moved to Jerusalem signaled the end of the battle for Jerusalem and the possibility of negotiating the city away from the Jews.

(Incidentally, if the rest of the world really wanted to contribute to peace, every country would move its embassy to Jerusalem. That would show the Arab world that their war is finished.)

That's also why so many Bible-believing Christians are pushing to get their countries to move their embassies to Jerusalem. For example, the Bible-believing Christians of Guatemala encouraged their government to relocate their embassy to Jerusalem. Jimmy Morales, president until January 2020, agreed and made this brave decision. This flurry of activity is happening all over the world, and if you map out where Bible-believing Christians live, you will hear calls to move the embassies to Jerusalem in those same places.

Another significant example is Brazil. The current president, Jair Bolsonaro, was elected by a base of evangelical Christians. He has made statements that he plans to move the Brazilian embassy to Jerusalem. Now, what does Brazil have to do with a city within a tiny country in the Middle East? But the president recognized that it was important, not only because he believes in the Bible but also because he understands that to maintain his political base, he needed to show them that he's also respecting Jerusalem. Bible-believing Christians around the world are pressing this issue because they believe that the restoration of Israel is part of the prophecy and they have chosen to support the Jewish state and to take part in the blessings that God promised.

The issue of Jerusalem has become important to Bible-believing Christians and Jews. And this trend will continue over the next few years. You will see that countries with Bible-believing populations will put more pressure on their governments to recognize Jerusalem. For them it's more than a political issue, it's a biblical one. As a result, these Bible-believing Christians are using their growing popularity to influence policy and push this biblical agenda.

The Jews' love of Jerusalem as their eternal capital stems from the Bible itself. The Holy City is referenced hundreds of times throughout Tanach. Jerusalem has been the capital of Israel since the time of King David, and for Jews (and Christians) it's important to rebuild Jerusalem as a fulfillment of prophecy. God planted the memory of Jerusalem in our DNA so that we'd never forget, and would long to return to our city and rebuild it.

Recognizing the importance of Jerusalem and its role in the fulfillment of prophecy is the core reason all those against Israel are working so hard to divide and destabilize it. To usurp the Jewish claim to this city, they revise history, change the maps for Mount Moriah to say Al-Aqsa, destroy evidence, and firmly deny Jews and Christians the right to pray at the site of the Holy Temple.

Uniting Jerusalem signifies the return from exile, as Judaism comes back to life. This represents the ultimate threat to Islam and those who actively reject the Bible. And so, the tension plays out in one small city that has been branded as the holiest place on Earth.

CHAPTER 10

The Existential Threat

The unholy alliance that is fighting to destabilize the Jewish state's military, economy, and world standing has been consistently refuted by Israel and her allies. But new tactics in the war of ideas have emerged. The focus of Israel's enemies has shifted to infiltrating the academic world and the media, partnering with organizations within mainline churches, and promoting the boycott, divestment, and sanctions movement. The underlying aim in all these activities is to delegitimize Israel and get people to treat Israel as a pariah.

After realizing that Israel is too strong to defeat militarily, these enemies turned their efforts to defeating it economically. If successful, they would then have a chance of destroying the Jewish state. As discussed in chapter three, Israel's high-technology boom and rapid economic development has been remarkable. The country has taken a market once limited to exporting fruits and vegetables and upgraded its industry to export an array of products based on scientific creativity and technological innovation. This was made possible by quality university education and an extremely competent labor force. Israel produces the second-highest number of computer chips in the world. Ten of the biggest global companies on the planet have their R&D centers in Israel.

The haters of Israel reasoned that attacking Israel economically through worldwide boycotts and sanctions would be the best way to cripple and ultimately defeat the only free democracy in the Middle East. Their plan, if successful, posed a real threat. Lacking natural resources and raw materials, Israel largely depends on imports and exports. Its high-tech industry powers the economy. This danger is compounded by the fact that it is surrounded by enemy states that refuse trade relations with the Jewish state. Therefore, Israel relies on trade with the Western, Asian, African, and Latin American countries to sustain a vibrant economy.

The soldiers of anti-Zionism operate in America under the banner of boycott, divestment, and sanctions, or BDS. Though its founders have worked hard to repackage their classic anti-Semitic agenda by using political terminology, the goal of the BDS movement is clearly anti-Jewish at its core.

BDS is based on the idea of pushing a blood libel against the Jewish people, painting them as occupiers of their own country and destabilizing any peaceful cooperation between Jews and Arabs. The movement has used not only economic weaponry against Israel but also worked to discourage cultural cooperation and continually spread misinformation.

On the financial side, we've seen several countries say that they're not going to work with Israel because of these false accusations of persecuting the Palestinian people. Some big conglomerates gave in to the pressure from the powerful Arab countries that they do business with. These companies surely thought that the decision not to work with Israel would upgrade their trade with the Arab states and even boost their sales.

We saw this with G4S, a British multinational security company that tried to divest from Israel. Another company that attempted to boycott places in Israel was Airbnb, an online marketplace where people can rent out properties to guests. The company unilaterally announced that it would no longer list about two hundred Jewish-owned properties in Judea and Samaria.

Luckily, these malicious attempts and others like them were thwarted as a result of the anti-BDS legislation that came out of South Carolina initiated by State Representative Alan Clemmons. The law states that the boycott, divestment, and the sanctioning of Israel is racism, and anyone participating in such activity can no longer do business with the state of South Carolina. This also bars state investment funds from investing in these banned companies. Florida passed a similar law, followed by Texas, and today twenty-seven states have adopted anti-BDS legislation.

The impact of such legislation is tremendous, because those states represent $3.5 trillion a year in trade and investment for any major company. Through legislation against racism, Israel has been able to thwart BDS. Airbnb reversed its decision to remove all Jewish rental listings in Judea and Samaria after a Florida legislator decided that state employees could not use Airbnb, and funds from Florida were unavailable for investment in the company as well.

The Israel Allies Foundation worked to help educate state legislators about the threat BDS posed to Israel, and the anti-BDS laws worked well as a deterrent to discrimination against Israel, especially because this legislation made it cost a lot to boycott Israel. Corporations were quickly faced with a decision: either bow to the pressure being imposed by Arab countries and anti-Semitic interest groups that don't want to work with Israel, or continue working with profitable states in America.

The laws have also provided an opportunity for companies that don't want to be involved in economic boycotts, but might be influenced or bullied into BDS, to say that they would like to join the anti-Israel alliance but unfortunately, they cannot do so because of this legislation.

Academic BDS

Another type of BDS is the academic boycott of Israeli universities and professors. Clearly inspired by the Nazis' laws, which forbade Jews from teaching or practicing medicine, this attempt to shut Israelis out of academia isn't even thinly veiled anti-Semitism. The BDS movement conducts events on campus called Israeli Apartheid Week, presenting the government of Israel as similar to that of South Africa during the apartheid era when institutionalized racial segregation forced nonwhite South Africans to live in separate areas, use separate public facilities, and attend different schools.

The libelous assertion that Israel is an apartheid state first arose at a 2001 UN-sponsored anti-Jewish diplomatic event, the World Conference against Racism, in Durban, South Africa. Activists in attendance were summoned to participate in the international demonization of Israel by calling it a racist state and declaring that Zionism is a form of racism. In 2005, the first Israeli Apartheid Week was held in Toronto, Canada, and in succeeding years was launched on campuses around the globe.

The bigoted event was permitted by university authorities in the name of academic freedom, and the propaganda war against the Jewish state continued to expand. Today, Israeli Apartheid

Week has become an annual event where university campuses host nasty protests against Israel and Jews and where Jewish students and advocates for Israel become targets.

Of course, the comparison between Israel and South Africa as far as apartheid has no basis in reality. The situation in Israel is completely different than that of South Africa during that time of racism and oppression. But those promoting this lie rely on the ignorance of most Americans, who know little about South Africa's history and about Israel. As we've already described, *all* Israeli citizens, regardless of race, religion, culture, or background, enjoy the same freedoms and are subject to the same rules and regulations.

Almost two million Arabs hold Israeli citizenship. They serve in the Knesset and on Israel's Supreme Court. Arab doctors and nurses work in Israeli hospitals. Arab and Jewish professors work together in Israeli universities. There are schools in Israel with both Arab and Jewish children. In fact, 22 percent of all medical students in Israel are Arab. There have been incredible success stories in the way that Israel has integrated the Arab population and their ability to have financial success and create good lives.

Another piece of the concocted apartheid analogy that doesn't align is the fact that most Palestinians don't live under Israeli control but under the violent authoritarian rule of the Palestinian Authority. In 2006, Palestinians *elected*, by majority, the Hamas terrorist organization, which opposes Palestinian statehood. Rather, its explicit aim is to establish an Islamic caliphate and destroy all of Israel. But that part doesn't often make the news.

This use of the term "apartheid" to describe Israel was a scheme not only to demonize Israel but to limit the ability of its supporters to defend the Jewish state. It also aimed to shift the attention away from the depravity of Israel's enemies. Using a title that immediately associates Israel with racial oppression has the effect of drowning out any criticism of the nation's enemies.

Anyone who dares to support Israel or condemn its enemies is liable to be ostracized. In 2014, Professor Andrew Pessin at Connecticut College posted a criticism of Hamas for its acts of illegal warfare against the people of Israel in the form of missile attacks *indiscriminately* sent over the border to murder and terrorize more than six million Jews who live within the range of Gaza's missiles. Seven months later, when the Facebook comment was noticed, Pessin was ostracized and subjected to continuous withering attacks by the Students for Justice in Palestine on campus. He even received death threats.[21]

At the University of Michigan, students who asked their professors for recommendations to study abroad in Israel were told that those recommendations would not be forthcoming simply because professors refused to recommend anybody to study in Israel. There are stories of Jews at other universities who needed to change the content of what they wanted to write about Israel in their papers so as not to be penalized with a bad grade.

In addition, campuses have been infiltrated by Islamic countries that have established chairs in these universities and imposed curriculum to teach anti-Israel propaganda. A student organization at New York University signed a pledge to participate in BDS, and they ostracized Jewish students who had joined pro-Israel organizations on campus along with other Jewish organizations operating in the city.

There's also been a push to ban Israeli professors from teaching in universities and to ban cooperation between Israeli universities and American universities, which is another horrible form of academic discrimination against the Jewish people. It's reached the point that anyone who wants to speak on behalf of Israel is booed and shouted out on campuses. Jewish students are constantly intimidated, not only for being supportive of Israel but just for being Jewish.

Today, if you're outwardly Jewish on campus, you're inevitably going to be ostracized and viewed as a pawn of the Jewish state. The academic BDS movement has created a dangerous atmosphere for Jews and Christian supporters of Israel on university campuses across America. Many American Jewish students are having to refrain from participating in pro-Israel activities due to this aggressive backlash.

These anti-Semitic activities are once again being challenged through legislation and other governmental action. One big success came in December 2019 when Donald Trump issued a presidential order saying that the federal government will review its funding to any universities involved in BDS and the promotion of this movement. It is likely that this executive order will produce a result similar to that which we saw from the anti-BDS legislation at a state level, and that colleges will no longer find it financially appealing to support the racist anti-Israel movement.

Universities that had their hands tied under the idea of free speech can now confront and label these activities as anti-Semitism and refuse to tolerate them. Until now, there has been a clear double standard wherein all other forms of racism were prohibited but anti-Zionism passed as free speech. Now, the notion that anti-Zionism is anti-Semitism has been adopted by the State Department and also by some European countries. Legislation and the presidential order are working to prevent the academic boycott of Israel that is being funneled through BDS on campuses.

Anti-Semitism in the Arts

The other type of anti-Semitism is cultural anti-Semitism. Pro-boycott activists push cultural isolation for Israel by enlisting artists such as Pink Floyd's Roger Waters and Elvis Costello to prevent other artists from performing in Israel under the guise of political reasons. They try to intimidate performers from being a part of any cultural Israeli experience. And they have had success influencing several singers, most notably Lauryn Hill from America, who in May 2015 canceled a concert in Israel just three days before she was scheduled to perform. BDS activists had launched an extensive social media campaign to put pressure on Hill.

The effort to prevent famous artists from performing in front of their fans in Israel has also aimed to prevent Jewish artists from performing in other countries. One of the prominent examples was the Jewish-American reggae singer and rapper Matisyahu, who was scheduled to perform in 2015 at one of Europe's largest reggae festivals in Spain. After pressure from BDS movements, the festival organizers asked Matisyahu to sign a statement endorsing a Palestinian state. When Matisyahu refused, he was disinvited.

Matisyahu is not an Israeli citizen; he is a Jewish-American. He does not have any influence on Israeli politics. No other participant in the festival was asked to clarify his or her political opinions in order to perform. And as the Federation of Jewish Communities in Spain pointed out in a statement: "It is noteworthy that the festival is not interested in the opinions of other participants on policies of Iran, the Islamic State, Syria, Hamas and Hezbollah."[22] This attempt to coerce the *one* Jewish artist into making political statements about Israel illustrates how BDS is not a movement meant to improve the lives of the Palestinians but is based in hatred toward Jews, and its goal is to destroy Israel.

Fortunately, after waves of criticism against the music festival organizers by the press, calling them out for discrimination, the organizers backtracked and apologized to the singer for canceling his appearance. They claimed that BDS groups used a campaign of "pressure, coercion and threats" against them. They then reinvited Matisyahu to perform. He agreed and bravely performed at the concert in front of thousands of fans despite a hostile environment of pro-Palestinian supporters waving flags and heckling him, once again orchestrated by the BDS movement.

For the most part, activists' attempts to harm Israel through cultural boycotts have been ineffective because of Israel's growing popularity as a venue for musical stars. Madonna, Paul McCartney, Justin Timberlake, and Lady Gaga have all recently performed in Israel. The Rolling Stones ignored pressure from Roger Waters and Nick Mason of Pink Floyd trying to get them to cancel their first-ever concert in Israel.

All these methods are failing, especially in America, because of their anti-Semitic nature and glaring double standards. They don't protest places like Syria, where around a million people have been murdered over the last five years, or Iran, where women are treated terribly and where there's no freedom of religion. But the BDS movement has managed to disguise its vicious motives to destroy the Jewish state in a garb of compassion for Palestinians and equal rights. This presentation has enabled them to appear credible and penetrate high society around the world.

In 2019 we saw this with Labour Party leader Jeremy Corbyn, who ran for prime minister in Britain. A fifty-three-page document submitted to the Equality and Human Rights Commission that year by the twenty-five-hundred-member Jewish Labour Movement (JLM) records numerous examples of anti-Semitic abuse within the party. "Since the time Jeremy Corbyn became leader," the document says, "he has made the party a welcoming refuge for anti-Semites." This was a scary time for Jews in England as it enabled someone who is anti-Jewish to hide his anti-Semitism behind the garb of politics. Had Corbyn been elected, we would have seen a mass exodus of Jewish citizenry from England to Israel, as we've seen with French Jewry leaving because of increasing anti-Semitism over the past decade.

In Europe people at rallies used to convey the message "I don't hate Jews; I am just critiquing Israel." But now we've witnessed a change back to traditional anti-Semitism, in which people are open about hating Jews, as with the Labour Party under Jeremy Corbyn. And we see this in a lot of different settings. Rallies that begin as anti-Zionist, with chants for "Free Palestine," quickly turn anti-Semitic, with participants calling "death to the Jews" and "from the river to the sea," an expression that calls for a Palestinian state in place of Israel.

This underlying anti-Semitism is personified in the BDS movement itself. BDS is not about peace or coexistence; it's not even about Israel giving up land to create a Palestinian state. The sole motivation behind BDS is the destruction of the Jewish *people*. It's about what the BDS participants call "anti-normalization." They don't want the existence of a Jewish state to become accepted. They don't want it to be normal for Jews to live securely in Israel. They want to apply BDS in Tel Aviv, in Jerusalem, and in Haifa because they want to *replace* Israel.

Unfortunately, precisely because of these movements that speak falsely in the name of freedom and human rights, any real opportunity for peace is threatened. What many people who buy in to the propaganda and join in the fight against Israel don't realize is that victims of BDS are, ironically, Arabs. The Barkan Industrial Area, located in Judea and Samaria, for example, has

146 factories that provide work for Palestinians. Thousands of Arabs and Jews work together in a great model of coexistence between the religions in the Middle East. These factories also allow Palestinians to increase their standard of living. They earn four times the salary they would make at the same job in the Palestinian Authority and are able to provide for their families.

But when these companies in Judea and Samaria are targeted by financial BDS, the Arabs suffer the most. If the owners of the companies are forced to move their operations to other cities in Israel as a result of discriminatory boycotts and product labeling, Palestinians lose their jobs, not Israelis. An unfortunate example of this boycott is the SodaStream company, which once employed both Jews and Arabs in a peaceful environment. The BDS movement implemented a merciless campaign that forced SodaStream to close its factory in Maale Adumim and move its operation to another location within Israel. As a result, five hundred Palestinians lost their jobs. But this was considered a win for the BDS movement.

Another example is the Israeli-owned supermarket chain Rami Levy, which has branches throughout Judea and Samaria. Three thousand Arabs are employed at these grocery stores, and several members of top management at the company are Arabs. But the BDS movement has targeted the stores and even called the Arabs who work there collaborators and traitors. It is important to note that these hateful campaigns are not coming from within the Palestinian communities that benefit from Israeli businesses in the area but from the external BDS movement largely operated from the United States and Europe.

In fact, when these business chains are targeted in an attempt to harm Israeli businesses, it's the thousands of Arab employees who suffer most.

The BDS movement was cofounded by Omar Barghouti, a prominent member of Hamas. This movement for justice and freedom, funded and pushed on campuses, is being promoted by a world-recognized terrorist organization. This isn't surprising given that the reason they're doing this is to destroy the state of Israel.

At the same time, the response from those who have recognized the true motives and worked to counteract the anti-Semitic movements has demonstrated the powerful cooperation between Bible-believing Christians and Jews. These groups have rallied against BDS and in the US have worked together to lobby their state representatives to pass anti-BDS and anti-discrimination legislation.

Unfortunately, a large and influential international body has chosen the wrong side in this battle and has endorsed the bigoted boycott of products produced by Jews in Israel. The European Union recently passed regulations requiring labeling of products produced by Jews in areas they specified as being made in "occupied territories." This includes products made in the heartland of the Jewish state: Judea and Samaria, as well as the Golan Heights and Jerusalem. The negative labeling is not required for products manufactured by Arabs in the same areas. When I addressed a session hosted in the European Union in December 2019, I told them this legislation is reminiscent of the Nazis' Nuremberg laws, which required Jewish goods to be labeled, and people were warned about buying from Jewish companies.

There are more than two hundred territorial disputes around the world. Morocco is occupying sub-Saharan Africa. Turkey is occupying Cyprus. Russia has occupied Crimea. The communities in the Arabic-speaking region of Iran have called themselves "occupied territories" since 1925 when Iran took over the area. Yet the members in the EU have turned a blind eye to these disputes and decided to focus their attention and regulation on *one* tiny strip of land. They have decided that goods produced in Israel must be labeled as "occupied" despite the fact that by international law these areas are considered disputed at best.

This is completely illegal according to the World Trade Organization, which has a policy that every single country must be treated equally. Therefore, if you want to label products made in Israel, you have to label products from the Moroccan sub-Saharan government as well as all the other countries with similar disputes. By passing this law, the European Union is violating the idea that you can't single out a particular religion.

But Jews and Christians are uniting to fight this anti-Semitic legislation. In 2019, twenty-five faith-based pro-Israel members of parliament from around the world joined in Jerusalem for the three-day Israel Allies Foundation's annual Chairman's Conference. They met with key political officials, attended workshops, and toured strategic areas in order to share ideas and projects aimed at furthering pro-Israel legislation, combating BDS and anti-Semitism, and countering the delegitimization of Israel in their home countries.

Much of the conference focused on responding to the recent European Union's Court of Justice decision requiring EU countries to label Jewish products from Judea and Samaria as having been made in "occupied settlements" instead of "Made in Israel." At the conclusion of the conference, the chairmen of the caucuses from each country all signed a referendum titled "Never again will nations stand silently in the face of boycotts against the Jewish people."

A coalition of ministers from European Union countries has risen up to fight the bias against Israel in the EU and in their own parliaments. We are going to see a significant change in policy coming out of England under the leadership of Boris Johnson, and I believe that Eastern European countries will follow suit. We will see this issue raised more frequently and more passionately, and the divide between those who hate Israel and those who support it will become more defined.

Iran

Of all the threats Israel faces, the most looming peril is a nuclear Iran. The website of Iran's Ministry of Foreign Affairs states explicitly that one of their official policies is to wipe the Jewish state off the map, and their supreme leader, Ayatollah Ali Khamenei, has repeatedly called Israel "a cancer that must be eradicated." This is the only case in the world today of a country that has openly stated that they want to destroy another country. To make matters worse, Iran has been working feverishly to develop the nuclear capacity to make this threat a reality.

Under the leadership of the radical ayatollah, Iran is advancing its plans through its rogue nuclear program and state-sponsored guerrilla terror groups (Hezbollah and Hamas) that have murdered thousands of innocent people. While lying to the Nuclear Energy Agency and naive world powers, Iran has been enriching uranium, and its sophisticated warheads now have the capability of reaching Tel Aviv and Haifa. Israel has taken Iran's repeated threats seriously and believes that the moment Iran has the nuclear capability, it will fire on the Jewish state.

Iran's aggressive nuclear program has become a source of incredible destabilization in the Middle East. Moderate Arab countries have expressed concerns that a nuclear-armed Iran would pose a threat to their security as well as Israel's. What makes Iran's nuclear ambitions especially troubling is the theology of the

Iranian leaders who truly believe that they are being directed by
Allah and that wiping out Israel would bring about the coming of
their version of the Messiah, the Twelfth Imam.

Iran's goal is not just to obliterate Israel but to dominate the
Middle East, and ultimately the world, in the name of Shiite
Islam. They've been successful in taking over large parts of Iraq,
Syria, and parts of Yemen. Iran's proxy army, Hezbollah, controls the government of Lebanon. Hamas, which is funded and
directed by Iran, controls the Gaza Strip. These proxy armies are
working to further Tehran's goal of wiping Israel off the map and
turning the world into an Islamic caliphate.

Iran's leaders believe that their nuclear program will begin
a chain of events that will allow them to take over the world.
Unfortunately, many Western politicians aren't aware of that theology and have attempted to negotiate with the Islamic Republic
of Iran. Its nuclear ambitions were given a huge boost by former
president Obama, who signed an executive order relieving Iran of
most of the sanctions that were crippling its economy and holding back part of its nuclear ambition. That 2015 deal is more
commonly known as "the worst deal in history" by the current
US and Israeli administrations. It cost the United States billions
of dollars and allowed Iran to continue working toward nuclear
breakout.

Obama and other world leaders entered the nuclear agreement
under the mistaken assumption that the Iranian government is an
honest broker and would uphold its end of the agreement. Even
if Tehran abided by the deal, it still allowed them to create nuclear
weapons within ten years of signing the deal. In addition to sanctions relief, Obama ensured that Iran received $150 billion up
front, enabling the rogue Islamic Republic to further its agenda
of spreading terror throughout the world. That money went to

terrorist organizations, it paid for weapons, and much of it was pumped directly back into Iran's nuclear program.

Obama's policy of engaging the Islamic world and making huge concessions to Iran allowed it to advance the nuclear program, but worse than that, he set Israel as a scapegoat. This is why Israeli prime minister Benjamin Netanyahu took the bold step of addressing the US Congress to plead his case in 2015. Unfortunately, the prime minister was treated hostilely by the Obama administration, and his message to Congress largely fell on deaf ears. Despite recognizing that Iran is first and foremost an existential threat to the State of Israel, the entire Middle East, and the world, policymakers who stand *against* Judeo-Christian values view a nuclear-armed Iran as an opportunity to intimidate and destabilize Israel.

But Israel's allies fought back. One of President Trump's first orders of business upon taking office was to reinstate sanctions against Iran and to sign an executive order effectively repealing the nuclear deal. He was able to do that because Obama never had the support of the Congress to pass this agreement. Once again, the world's leading state sponsor of terror is under intense scrutiny and is buckling under crippling sanctions. Even the nations that attempted to continue doing business with Iran faced sanctions from the United States.

Ultimately, Iran's plot to destroy Israel brought about a positive effect. The moderate Arab countries, who were viciously against Israel in the past, realized that they could no longer rely on American policy to help them deal with Iran. As a result, they needed to work with the other global forces in the Middle East, including Israel. Today, there is an unprecedented amount of cooperation between Israel and its Arab neighbors, including Egypt, Jordan, Saudi Arabia, and the United Arab Emirates. The threat of a nuclear-armed Iran and its entrenchment in the Arab states has forced them to turn to Israel as an ally with a common enemy. Despite the machinations of the past administration, Trump has been able to promise and deliver a rectified plan to stop the previous nuclear agreement – which would have been the most cataclysmic plan for the security and safety of Israel and the Western world.

CHAPTER 11

Religious Apartheid

Christians living in the Muslim world today are much like Jews of the 1930s in Europe. In the 1930s, Jews were attacked and persecuted while their neighbors and other nations watched in silence. Today, Christians are being persecuted, murdered, and annihilated in attempted genocides across the world. Yet the world remains silent, with few exceptions.

The myth of apartheid in Israel is clearly a false libel against the Jewish state, but no one around the world seems to care much about the real religious and gender apartheid that exists in countries under Muslim rule. Throughout the Middle East, from Iran to Saudi Arabia to Syria, Christians are regarded as second-class citizens. Many are murdered, forced to convert to Islam, or kicked out of their countries. This is happening daily. And one of the most shocking aspects of these atrocities is the lack of media coverage. People around the world know it's happening, but it's not being reported in the mainstream news.

The extent of this neglect can be seen during one of this decade's tragedies in Europe. On January 7, 2015, at about 11:30 a.m. CET local time, two militant Islamists stormed the offices of *Charlie Hebdo*, the French satirical weekly newspaper, in Paris. The two gunmen shot twelve people dead, including a French police officer, and wounded eleven others. This heinous attack sparked a wave of jihadist attacks across France, including the siege on the Hypercacher kosher supermarket, where a terrorist held nineteen hostages and murdered four Jews.

These brutal acts of savagery, right in the heart of Paris, prompted a huge response from European citizens, including demonstrations and candlelight vigils. One event that drew the attention of the world was the march of more than a million people through the streets of Paris to condemn terrorism. Yet on the same day in Nigeria, three hundred men, women, and children were slaughtered for the simple reason of being Christian. The Boko Haram Islamic terror group raided small villages and slaughtered every person; however, this catastrophic massacre targeting Christians was not reported in any of the world's leading newspapers.

So here you have attacks that made world news: an attack on a media site and an anti-Semitic act, which brought a million people to the streets. At the same time, there was the massacre of hundreds of Christian men, women, and children in Africa who were targeted for their faith, and the media all but ignored it. Why?

I think that a lot of the answer goes back to what happened in Israel, which is the tip of the sword. When there were suicide bombings in Israel, for example, few people said anything. When fifteen hundred Israelis were murdered during the Second Intifada, the world largely remained silent. Many even blamed Israel. They justified terrorist attacks by falsely accusing Israel of occupying land.

Then slowly, these types of events spread to other places in the world. People in America began to wake up to an incoming tide of violence with the September 11 terrorist attacks. We then saw Islamic terror attacks in Spain and in Mali. Concert halls, restaurants, shopping malls, and cafés were targeted. People began to take in the reality of jihadist attacks against civilians not just in Israel but throughout the world.

Christians continue to be persecuted and murdered around the world, and no one pays much attention or discusses it. And if they do, they often brush it off, saying, *Well, what are Christians doing there anyway? It's a Muslim country.*

And therein lies an important message: when people don't discuss or condemn what Jewish people in Israel must contend with as a result of Muslim terrorism, then when the same kinds of attacks spread to other places, people have a hard time condemning them. In short, it starts with the Jews but leads to the murder of others.

Muslims refer to both Jews and Christians as "the people of the book." Both religions are unwelcome in many Muslim lands. Islamists have a slogan in Arabic calling for the elimination of both faiths: "First the Saturday people, then the Sunday people." In other words, Islam will first target the Jews who celebrate Shabbat, and then the Christians who worship on Sunday. Such graffiti can sometimes be found in Muslim neighborhoods in the Middle East. It's part of their banter and their policies.

This ideology is apparent in Iran's nuclear program. Tehran has developed warheads that can reach Israel, but they are continuing to work on longer-range missiles that can reach northern Europe and even the US. Their plan is to annihilate Israel and the Saturday people first, then attack the Sunday people in Europe and the United States.

This process has occurred throughout the Middle East. The Saturday people have nearly vanished from Muslim lands where they used to have a community. More than a million Jews lived in Arab countries in the twentieth century. Most were forced from their homes after the creation of the State of Israel. Today just a few thousand Jews remain in the Muslim Middle East, mostly in Morocco and Tunisia. Now Islam has set its sights on the Sunday people, or Christians that remain in Arab lands. Due to the terrible persecution, Christians are fleeing at an alarming rate.

Christians Massacred around the World

Open Doors USA, a human rights organization that supports and raises awareness of persecuted Christians around the world, describes how Christians in Africa are suffering from oppression and are being mercilessly attacked by Islamic terror groups.[23] They are being cast out by their communities and murdered by Muslim leaders just for their faith.

The personal accounts that are surfacing daily are tragic. For example, in northern Burkina Faso (a country in West Africa), pastor Pierre Ouedraogo had spent forty years serving his church and community. Shortly after a prayer service in April 2019, a dozen men on motorcycles stormed the churchyard. They demanded the pastor and the five other congregants convert to Islam. When the pastor and congregants refused, the attackers gathered the men under a tree behind the church building, confiscated their Bibles and cell phones, then shot them all dead.[24] This is just one of many cases in that country involving attacks against Christians, who have been forced into hiding. Schools and churches have been closed, and thousands of Christians have fled to the south.

In the north of Nigeria, where Sharia law rules in twelve states, the minority of Christians likewise endure tremendous difficulties. In Nigeria's Middle Belt, Fulani militant herdsmen invade Christian villages, killing the men and kidnapping and raping women and children. In addition, Boko Haram and other sects (some of whom have pledged allegiance to the Islamic State) are responsible for the murder of more than a thousand people. In April 2019, twenty-five Christians were killed in a door-to-door murder spree. The group of Fulani raiders linked with Boko Haram has also expanded into neighboring countries.

In Mauritania, a country in northwestern Africa, Sharia law is enforced, citizenship is limited to Muslims, and converting from Islam is punishable by death. In East Africa, terror groups like al-Shabaab are attacking Christians. In the Horn of Africa, the government targets Christians, detains and imprisons them. In Somalia, Sharia law and Islam are protected in the country's constitution and Christians are violently persecuted. In Southern Ethiopia, armed mobs attacked churches, destroying property and possessions.

In Central Africa, internal conflicts within these countries continue to cause unstable governments, and extremist groups are using the unrest to brutally oppress Christians. In Rwanda, the government has closed thousands of churches. In the Democratic Republic of the Congo's eastern province of North Kivu, church leaders have been murdered. Thousands of Christians have lost their homes, and many have been forced to live in internal displacement camps.

In North Africa, Islamic oppression by both the government leaders and tribal communities continues to force Christians to convert. In Algeria, Egypt, Libya, Sudan, and Tunisia, Christians with Muslim backgrounds are pressured by their families to renounce their new faith. The Islamic State in Egypt has publicly declared a war on Christians.

But the violence and persecution of Christians in these poverty-stricken countries gets little attention in the Western world.

The Choice for Hatred

Christians were actually the pioneers of the modern ideologies throughout the Middle East. They were exposed to new values in Europe and attempted to bring these ideas back to the Middle East and introduce certain ideologies such as nationalism, patriotism, and later, socialism. The hope was to transform the environment of the Middle East from the original culture of tribalism and Islamism.

If successful, Christians would have possibly found their place as more equal and legitimate citizens in the Islamic world and would have been able to contribute to society in a more productive way. Instead, the Islamists dictated that Christians and Jews be forced to adopt an inferior social status known as *dhimmitude*. These minorities are marginalized and treated as inferior because they are non-Muslim. Rather than choosing equality, Islamic governments chose hatred and domination over the Jews and Christians of their countries, which continues today.

Presently, every country in the Middle East has at least a small population of Christians. These native Christians, most of whom speak Arabic and resemble the local population, face persecution and are alienated in these Islamic countries. Perhaps the most well-known crime against Christians is the ISIS-led genocide during the Syrian Civil War, in which more than a hundred thousand people were killed.

But among the least recognized or most commonly ignored areas of the Middle East where Christians are suffering are the ones controlled by the Palestinian Authority and Hamas. Christian Arabs living in these areas are the victims of frequent human rights abuses by Muslims. These violations include denial of employment, extortion, land theft, firebombing of churches, beatings, torture, kidnapping, and forced marriages. And Muslims who have converted to Christianity face the greatest danger.[25]

The PA has adopted Islamic law into its draft constitution. To abide by the sayings (hadith) of the prophet Muhammed, any Muslim who converts to Christianity is brutally oppressed and defenseless against Muslim cruelty. Tens of thousands of Palestinian Christians have fled their ancestral homes for other countries.

Jerusalem, Ramallah, and Bethlehem have always been the main cities of Arab Christian residences, but these areas have changed significantly in recent years. I previously detailed the Christian exodus from Bethlehem after the Palestinian Authority gained control over the city. What was once a thriving Christian city, the birthplace of Jesus, has become a Christian ghost town.

Israel remains an island of freedom for Christians in the Middle East. It's the only country in the region where the Christian population has *increased* since 1948 (and by more than 400 percent). Israeli security personnel guard Christian holy sites such as the Church of the Holy Sepulchre. But the enemies of Israel have attempted to blame Israel for the poor treatment of Christians by the PA and Hamas.

Justus Weiner, a human rights lawyer in Jerusalem, first became aware of the problems when a Christian pastor urged him to interview Christians in Palestinian cities. In his numerous publications, Weiner describes the difficulties Christian Arabs face while living under Palestinian rule. He also points to the ongoing decisions by international Christian leaders, such as leaders of American Episcopalians and some Presbyterians, to remain silent about the suffering of Palestinian Christians.

Rather than identifying the true Palestinian perpetrators, these churches have chosen to take the more politically correct path of pointing to the Israeli government without acknowledging or condemning Muslim violence. Nothing is said about the horrible suicide bombings, and they have yet to demand that Hamas recognize Israel, or renounce terrorism.

Deadly Silence

Christian persecution has reached an all-time high. Islamic terror groups such as Boko Haram target Christians, kidnapping women and children, forcibly converting them to Islam and selling them as child brides into slavery. These events are largely being covered up. Most of the killings reported in the news are painted simply as tribal conflict. But what they really involve is Muslims murdering Christians in Africa. The question is: Why are people not talking about that piece of the conflict? And why hasn't the international Christian community done anything to help their fellow Christians?

That international community has ignored the Islamic persecution and murder of Christians in northern Africa, the Middle East, and Asia. The United Nations has failed to condemn the Christian genocide by Muslims. It seems as if it has become politically correct to downplay murder and persecution if it is done in the name of Islam. Most Christians in America don't even speak about this crisis, and the churches have for the most part ignored it. The widespread silence on the matter is chilling.

Not only are Christians under attack physically in these far stretches of the world, they are under attack through religious persecution in America as well. Bible-believing Christians are being silenced and softly persecuted for their way of life, and no one is speaking up for them.

Slowly, the rights of Christians have eroded. Crosses have been ripped down in parks. Prayer has been removed from schools, and the ACLU seeks to strip the words "under God" from the Pledge of Allegiance. People object to the Ten Commandments being displayed in front of courthouses or public places. Any expression of religion, especially if it's a Christian symbol, is seen as threatening. Even wishing someone a merry Christmas can be perceived as hostile or intolerant.

While many try to justify their contempt for Bible-believing Christians as advocating for a separation of church and state, they display double standards regarding their tolerance for religious freedoms and education. Islam is often taught in high schools and universities, but Christianity is a forbidden subject in many classes. Behind this difference in standards is also the funding received from rich Muslim countries, which are buying chairs at universities and promoting education about Islam there. And to some extent, they've been able to silence the Christian world.

Another effort to silence Christians in America stems from the Johnson Amendment, which prohibits churches from publicly promoting or criticizing a political candidate and directly or indirectly intervening in a campaign. The legislation was named for America's thirty-sixth president, Lyndon B. Johnson, who first backed the amendment in 1954 while he was a US senator running for reelection. When a conservative nonprofit group advocated for his primary opponent, he introduced a revision to section 501(c)(3) of the federal tax code dealing with tax-exempt charitable organizations.

The practical application of this law threatens religious institutions with the loss of their tax-exempt status if they openly advocate their political views. Tax-exempt organizations cannot collect contributions on behalf of political campaigns. Clergy are forbidden to endorse or oppose candidates from the pulpit.

This also aids in the attempt to block churches from speaking out against the prejudice against the Christian religion and way of life. If, for example, a political candidate opposes the Bible or a religious monument being displayed in front of a courthouse, churches would naturally stand together and tell congregants to vote against that individual. But since the amendment prevents churches from even discussing politics, it effectively keeps churches from taking any political action for fear that the institution will lose its tax-exempt status.

Here too we see a double standard. While the amendment technically applies to all charitable organizations, it is mainly enforced against Christians. Planned Parenthood, for example, has tax-exempt status but joins political action committees that give millions of dollars to any political candidate who supports its ideals.

Today, there are several politicians who have made their way into the United States government and who embrace Sharia law. Recently, Representative Ilhan Omar abstained from a nearly unanimous House vote for a resolution recognizing the Armenian genocide, in which an estimated 1.5 million Armenian Christians were slaughtered in their villages. At the same time, she fights fervently for a boycott of Israel and has falsely accused the Jewish state of outrageous acts in order to enrage the public against it.

Atheists and radical liberals resent the alliance with Israel. When it comes to the Palestinians, they condone terrorism in the name of liberation and justice. But they speak of freedom *from* religion when it comes to Bible-believing Christians in America. Atheists and extreme leftists want to restrict the rights of Christians.

It's no coincidence that whenever you see hate against Israel, you also see animosity for Bible-believing Christians, because it is essentially a fight against those who defend God's covenant with Israel. The results are clear double standards when judging Israel and when it comes to the free speech of Bible-believing Christians in America. The people who are standing with Israel are being criticized and singled out when, in fact, they are the ones being persecuted.

Today, for the first time in history, these Christians are being lumped in with Jews because of their support for the state of Israel. In the past, Christians were seen as on the opposite side. As such, they were treated well. Now that they're on the side of Israel and the God of Israel, they've forfeited this privilege.

Over the ages, anti-Semitism emerged from a resentment of God's chosen people. Likewise, Bible-believing Christians, who are united with the Jewish people on the issue of Israel, provoke jealousy and contempt in claiming to be part of that covenant. And the same way that people didn't speak up when the Jews were being murdered, people today are not speaking up when Christians are being murdered. Instead they may say things like, *Christians are also promoting this colonial society.*

One of the reasons President Trump is so popular with the Christians in America is that he is willing to defend them. Many of these Christians observed former presidents and candidates who strongly identified as Christians yet failed to follow through with significant political action. In contrast, Trump has defended their rights.

While other politicians made big promises but then allowed the rights of Christians to be hollowed out, year after year, Trump is fighting for these Bible-believing Christians (as well as Jews). They, therefore, prefer a bold businessman in office – someone who knows how to fight – rather than a squeaky-clean altar boy who's a Bible-believing Christian but who remains quiet in the face of adversity.

President Trump has managed to achieve some historic wins. He's reforming the judiciary to once again provide freedom of religion. He doesn't shy away from mentioning God. He has supported a lot of initiatives that people in the Christian world care about. He has, for example, endorsed religious freedoms, and he's also doing tremendous good for Israel, which is so important to Christians. I believe this commitment to action is much of why he appeals to so many people.

CHAPTER 12

Gender Apartheid

The day following President Trump's inauguration in 2017, millions of women in Washington, DC and around the world marched to show support for women's rights and express opposition to the president's supposed attitude toward women. The activists donned obscene hats depicting women's genitalia and marched through the streets in what became possibly the largest single-day protest in American history.

One of the cochairs of the women's march was political activist Linda Sarsour. Oddly enough, Linda Sarsour is a Muslim who embraces Sharia law. As we've discussed, Sharia law is the most restrictive legal system in the world, especially concerning women. There is no ideology that demeans, degrades, and dehumanizes women as much as the principles of Sharia law. Women are considered the property of their husband or father. A woman can't own property, drive a car, can't vote, or go out in public unaccompanied. According to Sharia law, a man can beat his wife if she is disobedient or brings him shame.

Can a movement intent on advancing the universal rights of women allow someone like Linda Sarsour to be involved at such a high level?

Even more egregious is the fact that Sarsour has attempted to publicly defend Sharia law, arguing the system is positive. She claims that Muslim women actually prefer to cover their faces. She says that Muslim women don't want to go out in public or drive or vote, and she says that these freedoms are contrary to their culture. When confronted with the many denials of religious freedom and suppression of women in Sharia law, Sarsour casually dismisses the critical analysis, stating that Sharia law is misunderstood.

"You'll know when you're living under Sharia law," she writes, "if suddenly all your loans and credit cards become interest-free. Sounds nice, doesn't it?"[26] Instead of addressing the inequality for women, invasiveness into private lives, violations of human rights, and the rest of the freedoms that are sacrificed, she dodges the issue by saying that there will be interest-free loans, as if that benefit somehow overrides all the oppressive elements.

Perhaps the most alarming part of this scenario is not that someone can help organize the Women's March, *pretending* to be a feminist, while adhering to the most oppressive system for women, but that so many women in America put their trust in her.

Degradation of Women

Linda Sarsour and others who advocate for the BDS movement have made claims that Israel is an apartheid regime, but if we take a look at many of the countries that implement Sharia principles, we find a real form of apartheid: gender apartheid. Women are kept at home. They walk around covered in chador, a large piece of cloth that leaves only the face, or in some cases only the eyes, exposed. They don't have equal voting rights or status. In many of these places, gender inequality is compounded by the brutal subjugation of women. There are public beatings for women who show their face. Women can't drive cars. Women can't leave the house without chaperones. There's a prevalent culture of "honor killings" wherein women are murdered by their families after being raped or reported to have participated in an illicit relationship that is deemed anti-Islamic.

Hundreds of women are being kidnapped by Boko Haram. Yazidi women and girls are subjected to sexual slavery by the Islamic State in Iraq and Syria. Millions of women in Muslim countries have been subjected to genital mutilation. Innocent girls are forced to marry and become child brides. Indeed, the most intense "apartheid" (i.e., inequality) in the Middle East is gender apartheid.

In fact, the only place in the Middle East where women have equal rights and opportunities is Israel. Men and women serve in the army together. Women hold the highest professional and political positions as doctors, lawyers, engineers, and entrepreneurs. They have equal voting rights.

Yet Linda Sarsour and those who support her continue to speak on behalf of women's rights and represent Muslim women in America. They demonize Israel as an apartheid state and bash President Trump, while simultaneously defending a law that promotes worldwide threat and danger to women.

Without a doubt, we see a double standard presented by the Women's March organizers. By allowing an advocate for the suppression of women's rights to masquerade as an advocate for them, they have made themselves vulnerable to her pro-Sharia, anti-Semitic messaging.

A Look at Iran

Today in Iran, women are denied many basic human rights. They are forced to wear heavy clothing that covers them from head to toe. Women, even young schoolgirls, are required to wear the hijab in public, showing only their face – regardless of religion or nationality. Various institutions ensure the compliance to the Islamic dress code and other standards of conduct expected from women. Members of the police force also accost women considered to be wearing an improper hijab, even when they are inside their own cars.

Women living in the Islamic Republic cannot choose what to study in school, and they face discrimination in access to higher education. In 2012, gender-rationing measures were reintroduced in Iran. These rules exclude women from at least seventy-seven academic specializations. Women cannot attend sporting events, and many who have tried to enter stadiums have been detained.

The repression of women also applies to family life. Iran's civil code designates the husband as the head of the family and gives a husband authority over his wife in a variety of matters, including employment. Married women are forbidden from leaving the country without their husband's permission.

Husbands are also considered the main authority over children and hold sole legal guardianship of children. Girls and women, regardless of age, require the permission of a male legal guardian to marry for the first time. Child marriage is particularly common in some minority-populated regions, which leaves girls vulnerable to domestic abuse.

In addition to the restrictions on women's rights, there are alarming human rights abuses in Iran, which include restrictions on free speech. Iran has imprisoned many journalists, bloggers, and social media activists. An undesirable Facebook post can even cause someone to land in jail in Iran. And anyone who insults the supreme leader, president, or other government officials faces punishment.[27]

On January 3, 2020, President Trump made the decision to kill Qassem Soleimani, the head of Iran's elite Quds Force and all of Iran's regional and global terror apparatuses. Soleimani was responsible for assembling the largest terror network in history, which he used to implement Iran's imperialist ambitions throughout the Middle East. He provided aid to Hezbollah to take over Lebanon. He aimed hundreds of thousands of rockets at Israel. He indirectly controlled Syria, Yemen, and Iraq, which was responsible for ethnic cleansing and mass murder. He also killed hundreds of US troops.

Trump had expressed a desire to target Soleimani in 2017. Days before Soleimani was killed, his militants attacked the American embassy in Iraq. In January 2020, officials for the Trump administration told NBC News that the president had authorized the killing of Soleimani for his role in the killing of American citizens. This decision was backed by US Secretary of State Mike Pompeo.

The US airstrike that killed Soleimani in Baghdad also eliminated Abu Mahdi al-Muhandis, the commander of one of the Soleimani-controlled Shiite militias in Iraq. Iraqi protesters, who had been demonstrating against Iran's control over their government, claim that Soleimani ordered al-Muhandis to kill more than five hundred demonstrators in Iraq in 2019.

The airstrike should have been applauded by all those who advocate universal human rights and social justice. Yet some of the backlash in America, especially from liberals and feminists, was astoundingly hypocritical.

Ilhan Omar expressed outrage at the assassination of "a foreign official." American actress Rose McGowan tweeted an apology on behalf of the US saying "Dear #Iran, The USA has disrespected your country, your flag, your people. 52% of us humbly apologize. We want peace with your nation. We are being held hostage by a terrorist regime. We do not know how to escape. Please do not kill us."

McGowan has been at the forefront of Hollywood's #MeToo campaign. The movement was originally founded to help survivors of sexual assault and, according to McGowan, has helped society to have less tolerance for abuse of power. Yet she apologized for the assassination of one of the most powerful men in the Islamic Republic, a barbaric regime against women.

So how can someone be an activist for the #MeToo movement and care deeply about the oppression of women, and yet support a man who was one of the worst abusers of women in modern history?

Another startling example of the moral blindness that is plaguing liberal America is the widespread media support of Colin Kaepernick. This former NFL quarterback, who became increasingly popular after his kneeling during the national anthem at football games, publicly denounced America's strike on the terrorist Soleimani by writing on Twitter that "There is nothing new about American terrorist attacks against Black and Brown people for the expansion of American imperialism."[28]

His response is a classic demonstration of how twisted people's logic can be, displaying a new height of ignorance and immaturity in a generation of millennials. In his eyes, a targeted strike on a military official who was organizing terror against innocent civilians across the Middle East is considered a "terrorist attack" while the actual terrorist is painted as the victim. The most absurd display of his unfamiliarity with the ruthless Iranian terrorist is the fact that Kaepernick brought race into his complaint against America, without considering that the man he was defending was viciously torturing and killing black and brown people.

Such careless complaints about sensitive military operations illustrate how when someone's moral compass is broken, it points them in the opposite direction of recognizing truth. That is not to say there is no problem of racism in America or that claims of police brutality are unfounded, but rather that declaring faults with any country must be put in a proper historical and global perspective, without adopting double standards. Here is a man who achieved every luxury of the American dream. He became a multimillionaire because of the freedoms, opportunities, and economic success that his country offered. Yet while speaking out against the social injustice, labeling America as an imperialist nation, Kaepernick proudly wears a shirt with a picture of Fidel Castro – the Cuban dictator who ruthlessly imprisoned and murdered thousands of his people, broke up families, and denied an entire generation basic political freedoms. Had Kaepernick been living in Cuba under Castro and criticized the government in the same manner, he would surely have been punished severely.

And how was Kaepernick punished in America for his demonstration during the national anthem and criticism of the government? Nike decided to endorse him, and celebrities rushed to his defense. These responses, while paradoxically highlighting the freedoms in America in contrast to other nations, are a clear example of how illogical certain people have become and their inability to make proper moral distinctions.

The Response of the West

This problem is broader than a few politicians and activists, who seem to believe in women's rights only when it suits them. Why, in general, is there no response from the West against what's happening to women in the Middle East?

While liberal movements in America find every opportunity to obsessively criticize Israel for human rights violations, they remain silent about and even tolerate the persecution of women and minorities in Muslim countries. Why, for example, are there no women's marches for the 270-plus women who were kidnapped in Boko Haram, or the Yazidi women and girls subjected to sexual slavery, or the two hundred million women who have been subjected to forced genital mutilation? Why don't liberal activists complain about how women are treated in Saudi Arabia, which is proud of its ideology that basically enslaves the country's women? How do they turn a blind eye to the violations of rights in the Muslim world when they are supposedly in favor of universal rights? Why are the members of the extreme left allowing a woman who embraces Sharia law to guide them? Women are being oppressed, tortured, raped, genitally mutilated, and stripped of all their rights, yet the feminist movements are ignoring it. There's no Gender Apartheid Week on campuses. There's no proposed legislation against it.

While many Jews in the former Soviet Union and its satellite nations during the Cold War were forbidden to practice their religion and prevented from immigrating, US president Gerald Ford in 1975 signed into law the Jackson-Vanik amendment (an addition to the Trade Act of 1974), created to put pressure on the Soviet Union for human rights abuses. In order to receive economic benefits in trade relations with the United States, communist economies needed to comply with free-emigration policies. For many Jewish communities in America, a politician's endorsement for this amendment served as a litmus test for US commitment to Soviet Jewish emigration.

Why wouldn't feminists suggest similar legislation to these Muslim countries, saying *If you abuse women and treat them like property, then we're not going to do business with your countries*? And why, in international bodies for rights of women, are these extremely oppressive countries being allowed to serve on the committees? To this day, Iran has a seat on the UN council for the rights of women.

How is it that people whose political identity is based on equality and human rights are failing to recognize and fight for an entire group of oppressed and abused women? Rather, they have chosen to implicitly accept the abuse of women in Muslim countries. Liberal atheists sit at the same table with radical Islamists, virulent anti-Semites, and supporters of Sharia law at political conventions and college campuses. We are witnessing the selective alliance of "the enemy of my enemy is my friend."

What we are seeing today is, in many ways, an illustration of the warning of Isaiah the prophet: "Woe unto them who call evil good, and good evil; who present darkness as light and light as darkness; who present bitter as sweet, and sweet as bitter!" (Isaiah 5:20).

At the heart of the clash of civilization is a struggle between biblically based morality and moral relativism. The ability to effectively distinguish between right and wrong requires a source other than instincts or culture. For believers, the Bible is the source that teaches what's right and wrong, good and evil. But when the ability to determine good from evil is up to a culture or feelings, there is no true measuring stick.

What we are seeing today is that the political agenda determines which moral framework is used. When it comes to condemning Israel, "equal rights" becomes the absolute concern and a means to gain power. But when it comes to condemning the oppression of women in the Muslim world, the agenda pushes for value pluralism and moral relativism: what's wrong in the eyes of one culture is right for another; there is no objective moral system that we all should live by. And the driving force behind this selective viewpoint, in any given context, is the rejection of the Bible and of God.

For this reason, we see the bizarre situation where feminist movements partner with individuals who defend Islamic doctrines suppressing women. Mainline churches work together with a woman who supports the same Islamic regimes that murder people just for being Christian. And pluralist multiculturalists *defend* Islam from the same critical examination that should be applied to any religion in a modern, free society, and attempt to block free speech.

Many criticisms of Islamic culture come from Muslims or ex-Muslims. Ayaan Hirsi Ali, for example, was raised as a Muslim, went through genital mutilation at age five, and fled from an arranged marriage, seeking political asylum in the Netherlands. She became a member of its parliament after renouncing Islam, and later moved to the US after receiving death threats. But because she now points to the brutal treatment of women in Muslim societies and calls for reformation of inhumane laws, she has received hostile treatment from Linda Sarsour and other Muslims, and her lectures were boycotted at universities.

Behind all these contradictions and seemingly strange partnerships is a shared rejection of God and the Bible. The further they get away from the source of right and wrong, the more likely they are not only to abandon essential values but also to hate Israel. It's also why we find extreme liberal Jews blatantly disregarding the security of Israel, suggesting solutions that would essentially be suicidal for the Jewish state. Bernie Sanders, for example, a Jewish candidate in the 2016 and 2020 Democratic presidential races, has aligned himself with and praised activists like Linda Sarsour and Congresswomen Ilhan Omar and Rashida Tlaib, all of whom have a long history of anti-Semitism. At the same time, he fails to condemn Hamas for terrorism and for the treatment of their own people, yet freely calls Israeli prime minister Netanyahu a racist, and labeled the American Israel Public Affairs Committee as a platform for bigotry without explaining his position.

How could he embrace an Islamist anti-Semitic woman who supports Sharia law? The answer is that although Sanders was born Jewish, he's adopted the Western liberal mentality that all moral judgments are subjective, while rejecting the moral compass of the Bible.

We can also see this trend playing out in the policies that people support. Today, 90 percent of the Reform Jews in America are against President Trump, whereas more than 90 percent of Orthodox Jews in America support him. Put simply, the degree of one's religious ideas and how closely someone adheres to the commandments of the Bible determines whether they will uphold a constant standard of right and wrong.

The further someone moves away from Biblical values, the more the lines of right and wrong become blurred. Human rights in one context are thrown out in another. As it manifests in political views, the further away from the source one travels, the more likely they are to irrationally reject the policies of President Trump and to fight against Israel.

The real reason there is no rejection of this horrible gender apartheid in the Middle East is that there is no moral compass: a firm sense of right and wrong stemming from the Bible.

PART 4
TRUMP IN ACTION

CHAPTER 13

The Trump Doctrine

The golden era of Jewish sovereignty in Jerusalem that peaked during the reign of King Solomon – whose Hebrew name means "peaceful" – represented a time of tranquility in the Holy Land. There were no wars or internal conflicts. Under his rule, the Jewish kingdom prospered, stretching from the river of Egypt in the south to the Euphrates River in the north. It was acknowledged and respected by neighboring rulers.

King Solomon's greatest achievement was the construction of the Temple (Beit Hamikdash) in the capital city. The Holy Temple, serving as the center of Jewish life and a sign of spiritual glory, stood for more than four hundred years in the heart of Jerusalem. But in 586 BCE, the king of Babylonia, Nebuchadnezzar, marched into Jerusalem, pillaged the city, and destroyed the Temple. He deported tens of thousands of Jews to Babylon. It looked like the end of the Jewish story.

Many of the exiles were traumatized by the shock of Jerusalem's fall, and the future of the Jewish people was uncertain. Some Jews began to lose hope of a future redemption, while others made great attempts to remember Zion and Jerusalem. The opening verse of Psalms 137 relates the devastation felt during this time: "By the rivers of Babylon, there we sat down and wept when we remembered Zion." The later verses convey the commitment to never forget Jerusalem.

During the period of Babylonian captivity, Ezekiel shared his prophetic visions of the heavenly chariot and the eternal temple, telling his people that God would never forsake them or allow them to assimilate. He revived the dry bones in the valley of Dura, symbolizing the rejuvenation of the Jewish people.

Although this exile was very traumatic, the Jewish people adapted, set up institutions of study, and thrived in Babylonia. In 539 BCE, the Persians overthrew the Babylonian Empire – an event that, seen through the eyes of the Bible, was considered divine retribution for attacking Israel. Shortly afterward, a Persian emperor arose, known in world history as Cyrus the Great. In the sixth century BCE, Cyrus embarked on a mission of conquest. In only three decades, he was able to establish the foundation of the most extensive empire known, a dominance that would stretch from the borders of India to Greece, down to Egypt and Ethiopia, and up to modern-day Russia. More than thirty nations came together under this great king, who declared himself to be "King of the World."

Despite his great power, Cyrus showed mercy to the Jewish people and allowed them to return to their homeland and rebuild their Temple. He even funded their efforts. After seventy years of exile in Babylon, Jews once again worshipped God in the Holy City of Jerusalem. This restoration marked a new era in the history of Israel, the period of the Second Temple.

For this reason, Jewish history likewise reveres Cyrus. He is mentioned in the prophecies of Isaiah, in the book of Ezra, at the end of 2 Chronicles, and in the book of Daniel (1:21; 6:29;

10:1), wherein he appears as the leader destined to save the people of Israel and help it to fulfill its purpose on behalf of the God of Israel.

> Now in the first year of Cyrus king of Persia, at the completion of the word of the Lord by the mouth of Jeremiah, the Lord stirred up the spirit of Cyrus king of Persia, that he issued a proclamation throughout his kingdom, and put it also in writing, saying: "So said Cyrus king of Persia: All the kingdoms of the Earth the Lord God of the heavens has given me; and He has commanded me to build Him a House in Jerusalem, which is in Judea." (Ezra 1:1–2)

> Thus said Cyrus, king of Persia: "The Lord, God of Heaven, has given me all the kingdoms of the Earth, and he has commanded me to build Him a Temple in Jerusalem, which is in Judah. Whoever there is among you of all His people – may God be with him and let him go up." (2 Chronicles 36:23)

Two hundred years before Cyrus was born, Isaiah predicted King Cyrus' rulership, mentioning him by name. He predicted that he would be the man who would liberate the Jews from Babylonian exile and return them to Jerusalem: "So said the Lord to His anointed, to Cyrus, whose right hand I held, to subdue nations before him, and to loosen the loins of kings; to open the doors before him, and the gates may not be shut" (Isaiah 45:1).

Cyrus, destined as the one to punish destroyers of the Temple, opened the portals of the gates of Babylon to the Jews. And throughout the millennia of catastrophes that followed for the Jewish people, Cyrus served as the symbol of the moral gentile ruler who would enable the ultimate return of the Jewish people to the land of Israel, the restoration of their nationhood, and security against their enemies.

Those who visit Jerusalem today understand that it's not an ordinary city. Every step is a journey through Jewish history. From this perspective, it is important to understand that any policy concerning Jerusalem, the city's borders, or changes in the control of certain areas is seen in the broader context of the Jewish struggle. Whenever a leader is good to the Jewish people, it is only natural to put them in this historical framework.

The ability to look at Israel through a biblical lens had been a recurring theme in American history. After the Jewish fight for statehood, President Harry Truman was faced with a dilemma of whether to support Israel. Almost all his advisors, including his secretary of state, told him not to recognize the new Jewish state. Arab oil, they explained, was the main priority because a war with the Soviet Union was looming. It would, therefore, be unwise to recognize Israel. In 1948, as the British Empire withdrew, five Arab nations sat on the border, ready to invade Israel. Though the Arabs already possessed twenty-two countries of their own, they wanted Israel too.

Politically, Truman was under tremendous pressure. In the end, he made the momentous choice to sign an executive order recognizing the State of Israel, within eleven minutes of its founding. When he was later thanked and credited with helping to create the State of Israel, Truman responded, "What do you mean, 'helped to create'? I am Cyrus. I am Cyrus." This comparison to Cyrus was not an attempt at self-aggrandizement – it was rooted in his understanding of scripture.

Before the 2016 presidential election in the United States, some evangelical Christians began comparing candidate Donald Trump to King Cyrus. The comparison is that a nonbelieving leader can be used by God to enact policies that advance the interest of believers, in this case, Christians and Jews. And it's not surprising that when President Trump does something good for the Jewish people and for the world, he is brought into the historical chain. When Trump declared Jerusalem as Israel's capital, for example, Prime Minister Netanyahu likewise equated him to Lord Balfour, Harry Truman, and the original symbolic acts of Cyrus the Great.

Biblical versus Political

Cyrus looked at the Jewish people differently and decided to change the course of history. After their Temple was destroyed, the Jews had been dispersed, kicked out of the land of Israel, and brought to Babylon as captives. The nation under which they lived could now do with them how they pleased, making them into workers or even slaves. But Cyrus didn't see their plight through a realpolitik lens. Instead, he looked through a biblical lens. He recognized the wrong that had been done and decided to take a completely different path, allowing the Jewish people to return to their land in Israel and even helping to fund the rebuilding of the Temple.

Some may say, how can that be? He was a Persian king who didn't know anything about Hebrew scripture or prophecy. Many believe that his viewpoint toward the Jewish people was inspired directly by God – as indicated by the prophets, the restoration of Israel to their land and Temple was destined to happen through him. This powerful ruler started looking at everything from a biblical perspective, which is why he decided to bless the Jewish people by helping them regain sovereignty in their land. These actions were driven by compassion for a conquered people, and as an attempt to rectify the mistreatment of the Jews in Babylon by the previous king. This is also why Persia was blessed at the time.

I am not saying that Cyrus acted selflessly. Rather, he realized that what the Babylonians were doing to the Jews was against the Bible, and he didn't want to be on the wrong side of history. He wanted God's blessings, not curses. Cyrus wisely adapted his policy to act according to the Bible. Politically, it would have perhaps been smarter to leave the Jews in Babylon, not to fund their religious aspirations to reestablish a Temple. It brought nothing to him. And it likely wasn't a popular move internally. But he did it because he wanted to be on the right side of history.

It is easy to understand decisions that act in one's best interest politically, but when a ruler makes an unpopular decision – knowing that it will come with plenty of backlash – it begs a deeper investigation into the cause. In cases when a decision is made to stand with Israel, it becomes clear that the leader in question is being divinely inspired.

Like Cyrus, President Trump looks at Israel from a biblical point of view. He understands how the base of his voters looks at Israel, and when Bible-believing Christians voted for him, they made it clear that they wanted him to improve relations with Israel. Trump changed the course of America's policy toward Israel, drastically altering the trajectory set by past presidents. He used the fact that his base was behind him to implement major policy shifts. These shifts were not necessarily politically correct, but they were biblically correct.

Since former president Carter, the US's Middle East policy had viewed Israel's "occupation" as responsible for the absence of peace in the Middle East. The PLO's aggression and refusal to either disavow terrorism or accept Israel's right to exist were brushed aside. The Obama administration adopted the 1978 Hansell Memorandum, which condemned Israeli communities in Judea and Samaria, as US official policy. This State Department document was based on an erroneous interpretation of the Fourth Geneva Convention from 1949 and had no basis in international law. But Obama's acceptance of it enabled the UN Security Council to pass a resolution criminalizing Jewish communities beyond the 1949 armistice line.

The Trump administration recognized the false narrative, and Secretary of State Mike Pompeo announced that the administration was replacing the Hansell memo with an accurate assessment of international law. "It is important that we speak the truth when the facts lead us to it. And that's what we've done," Pompeo announced in January 2020. President Trump's policies expose the corrupted narrative of his predecessors' policies toward Iran and Israel.

Trump ended the Obama doctrine on Israel. He stopped blaming Israel for the problems of the Middle East, and he started looking at how to strengthen the alliance between Israel and America. He refocused the story by seeing the situation as it is: that Israel is a small but flourishing democracy amid the hostile Middle East. This shift in perspective has allowed America and Israel to once again work together in harmony.

Because many of Trump's core supporters are Bible-believing Christians who look at the world from a biblical point of view, he adopted their perspective and as a result made some bold decisions. The most notable example is moving the US embassy to Jerusalem. Every advisor, from the secretary of state at the time to his secretary of defense, told Trump that he was making a huge mistake. The State Department said that such an initiative would start a third Intifada and that thousands would be killed. It could lead to World War III.

Even the Democrats who voted for the Jerusalem Embassy Act told him that it was not the right time, that such a move would cause incredible destabilization in the region. For this reason, other countries did not want to move their embassies. They feared the reaction by the Muslim world. Moving the embassy did not seem to be a smart political decision. But because Trump's base is Christian and expected him to do the biblically correct thing, rather than the politically correct thing, he did it. And that led to a huge policy shift.

All the explosive reactions that people worried about never happened. And this has been the general counterintuitive trend. Decisions made solely from a political perspective, in the name of peace but at the expense of Israel's security, end badly. For example, the evacuation of all Israeli troops and civilians from the Gaza Strip in 2005 only brought more violence and heartache. Jews had lived in Gaza since biblical times. Throughout the 1980s, new communities were established. Yet the Israeli Cabinet, in an attempt at peace, unilaterally disengaged from the Gaza Strip in 2005.

In the Israeli settlement of Gush Katif, 8,600 residents were forcibly removed. More than twenty Jewish communities – homes, shops, manufacturing sites, and synagogues – were demolished, along with a greenhouse that yielded 90 percent of Israel's organic produce. The heartbreak of the expulsion took a serious toll on the displaced community yet was justified as a pilot test that would lead to further disengagement for the sake of peaceful coexistence between Palestinians and Israeli neighbors. Instead, Israel only suffered more as a result. The massive evacuation from Gaza enabled Hamas to strengthen itself, and that territory has become a constant source of instability. The former Jewish villages were turned into terrorist training camps. The area became a launching pad for thousands of rockets aimed at Israeli civilians. Hamas leader Yahya Sinwar, who recently threatened to "crush Tel Aviv," boasted how irrigation pipes left after the disengagement were used to manufacture rockets.

But when decisions are made looking from a biblical point of view, things go right. People later realize that the threats were never followed through and their fears were unfounded.

The Issue of Jerusalem

Moving the United States embassy from Tel Aviv to Jerusalem is the boldest move by President Donald Trump and the most important thing he could have done for Christians and Jews. There are many key issues for Christians and Jews, but the issue of Jerusalem tops the list.

In addition to the importance of Jerusalem historically, this city is most important because it is the place where the next stage of prophecies will be fulfilled. From a Jewish perspective, God is bringing the people of Israel back to the land that was promised to their forefathers Abraham, Isaac, and Jacob. The major prophecy yet to be fulfilled is the coming of the Messiah (Mashiach in Hebrew) and the rebuilding of Jerusalem. This will lead to the messianic age, when all people will come to recognize the Creator. Then there will be peace, and everyone will then be free to devote their attention to the knowledge of God. But if we give away Jerusalem, it will inevitably impede this process.

One may wonder: *Why do Bible-believing Christians care about Jerusalem?* Christians also believe that the Messiah will return to Jerusalem, setting the stage for a change in the world. The result is that two sides have formed. On one side there are people with Judeo-Christian values, while the other side involves people against those values who don't want to see those prophecies fulfilled.

Because Jews and Christians both see Jerusalem as crucial to the future redemption, they are working together to keep it united under Jewish control. For them, control of Jerusalem is not a political fight to possess more territory, it's a biblical issue. And President Trump moved the embassy to Jerusalem because he realized that this was one of the most important issues from a biblical point of view. He wanted to show them that, unlike previous politicians, he follows through on his promises.

The focus on recognizing Jerusalem as the capital of Israel is not new. In 1995, the US Congress adopted the Jerusalem Embassy Act, which called for the relocation of the embassy to Jerusalem and the recognition of Jerusalem as Israel's capital city. The act passed in the House of Representatives by a bipartisan majority of 374 to 37 and was reaffirmed by an almost-unanimous vote in the Senate of 93 to 5.

Yet for more than twenty years, every president has used the law's waiver, declining to follow through with the provisions of the act. Every six months for the entirety of their terms, every president from Clinton to Bush to Obama would sign a waiver delaying the relocation of the embassy to Jerusalem for security reasons. They believed that postponing the recognition of Jerusalem was better for peace, a judgment based on politics.

The reason no one had the courage to do it is that they were looking at it from a political point of view. Politically, it would cause more conflict than it would do good. But after signing the waiver twice in 2017, President Trump, just like Cyrus, ignored the political point of view and acted out a biblical point of view. Understanding that biblically it was right, in 2018 he determined it was time to officially recognize Jerusalem as the capital of Israel. Acknowledging Israel as a sovereign nation with the same right as any nation to choose its own capital, he explained, was "the right thing to do."

Moving the embassy had an immense effect in the region and around the world and brought the prospect of peace closer. Although it was a pressing issue for decades, when Christians made the issue of Jerusalem a priority through the Republican platform for Israel, it came to fruition. Here we can see the remarkable results of faith-based diplomacy, an illustration of just how important people of faith are in the political process in general and specifically to President Trump.

Scouting Out the Land

Once, while I was visiting the US embassy in Jerusalem, Aryeh Lightstone, the chief of staff for the ambassador to Israel, David Friedman, took me to the ambassador's office. I immediately noticed a massive painting on one of the back walls. It first caught my attention because the office is small. And the content of the portrait is very clear to anyone familiar with the Bible. It captured the moment when the twelve spies come back from scouting the land of Israel after forty days.

The men chosen by Moses were the heads of each tribe, sent to gather information about the entrance into the land. Yet all but two came back with discouraging reports that instilled fear in the hearts of the Jewish nation, saying, "We are unable to go up against the people, for they are stronger than us... In our eyes, we seemed like grasshoppers, and so we were in their eyes" (Numbers 13:33). It is regarded as one of the most tragic biblical episodes.

As despair spread through the people of Israel, Joshua and Caleb spoke up to renew the faith in the original plan: "The land which we passed through to spy it out is an exceedingly good land. If the Lord desires us, then He will bring us into this land and give it to us, a land which flows with milk and honey" (Numbers 14:7–8).

The painting depicts the giant fruits, branches with clusters of grapes, pomegranates, and figs, and the Mishkan (sanctuary) in the desert. The ten spies are depicted with solemn expressions of fear, while the two courageous and worthy spies, Joshua ben Nun and Caleb, stand on the side.

Looking at the painting, I remarked to Aryeh about how I found it strange that such a scene would be chosen as the visual centerpiece for the office of the ambassador.

To the best of my memory, he replied, "This represents the policy of the Trump administration. We're not going to do something because everyone says we need to do it, advising us that you're going to lose, or be killed for being loyal to the Bible. We're going to do what's right. And we believe that if God is with us, no one can stand against us. And that's also why we moved the embassy. This was a past miscarriage of justice, concessions made for political considerations, but we're going to change that approach and do what we believe is right regardless of all the naysayers."

That message resonated with me because it follows the historical theme I had been witnessing. Many people look at things from a political point of view, and when they try to implement these policies to achieve stability, everything backfires. At Camp David, they have cocktail parties and toss around slogans about "land for peace." Everyone is happy and hopeful. And then, as a result, Israel is ruthlessly attacked with rockets and bombings for years. When leaders look only through a political lens, more people die; the only path to success is when they do what's right biblically.

The minute you act from a biblical perspective, good things happen. Christians and Jews who believe in the Bible understand this, and that's why we are working together for Israel. And because the president has surrounded himself with people who look at world events through a biblical lens – Christians such as Vice President Mike Pence and US Secretary of State Mike Pompeo and observant Jews such as Jared Kushner, Jason Greenblatt, and Ambassador David Friedman – Trump's policies are being shaped accordingly. And that's why they're working.

This leads us to the horrible regime of Iran, which oppresses its people. Its official foreign policy is to wipe Israel off the map. There is no freedom of religion and no gender equality, and Tehran has a long history of aggression toward the United States.

In her January 2020 article in the *Jewish World Review*, "Donald Trump and the Mythmakers,"[29] Caroline Glick outlines two contrasting approaches that have guided American Middle East policy for decades and explains what she calls a shift to "reality-based politics" in the current administration. The foreign policy of past US presidents has been to appease the Islamic Republic rather than to take a strong stand against it. In November 1979, soldiers of Iran's dictator Ayatollah Khomeini seized the US Embassy in Tehran and held fifty-two Americans hostage for 444 days. Iranian revolutionaries cursed Americans as imperialists, and Khomeini's followers shouted, "Death to America." The Carter administration chose not to fight back.

As president, Ronald Reagan "turned a blind eye to Iran's responsibility for the terror attacks…against the United States – including the bombing of the US embassy in Beirut in April 1983 and the bombing of the Marine barracks in Beirut in November 1983," Glick said. She lists how successive presidents continued much the same stance concerning Iran: During the Iraq War from 2003 to 2011, "Iran organized the Shiite militias that waged war against the US forces in Iraq. It also supported Al-Qaeda in Iraq.… More than six hundred American forces were killed…in attacks carried out with Iranian-made explosive devices." Glick points out that "rather than confront Iran for its aggression, the Bush administration tried to make a deal with the mullahs."

Reaching an agreement with Iran became the main goal of US foreign policy during the Obama administration, at the expense of Israel. He approached the situation from a political standpoint and tried reasoning with the evil Iranian regime. He thought that sending them money, buying them off, and negotiating a sweetheart nuclear deal would allow them to keep their dignity and would encourage them to deal fairly with the United States. Instead, his policy led to the spread of terror, the death of two million people through the so-called Arab Spring, which sparked wars across the Middle East, and to more instability in the region.

The Trump administration changed US policy toward Iran. It could not allow compromises at the expense of American values, the lives of innocent people, and the safety of Israel. President Trump recognized that the Iranian government is doing terrible things to its own people, they are training proxy armies in Lebanon, Syria, Iraq, and Yemen, and they are trying to kill Americans and destroy Israel.

The administration's decisions marked a shift from the political doctrine to a Judeo-Christian doctrine. Once again, it's having incredible results. People are inspired by the fact that Trump is keeping his word by upholding the values of freedom, democracy, and justice that he has absorbed from his Christian supporters and is using those values to guide policy in Iran. The strength of the United States' new approach has also empowered citizens in Iran, who are now standing up for their rights, protesting the government that's been oppressing them. In January 2020, hundreds of protesters walked around US flags that the regime had painted on the pavement, instead of trampling on them, to show their respect for America. The Trump doctrine of looking at things from a biblical point of view, from a moral perspective, is having real effects on the ground in Iran as well.

CHAPTER 14

Defending the Covenant

One of the notable changes in this generation is the increase in Jews and Bible-believing Christians who are recognizing the covenant between God and Israel. Even more amazing is how they are working together across the globe to protect this covenant through faith-based diplomacy. Faith-based diplomacy is becoming one of the most positive forces in politics today. It is arguably the most effective tool in Israel's diplomatic arsenal because it enables people of faith to get involved in the most critical issues concerning the country.

Productive and meaningful diplomatic activity, inspired by people with deep religious convictions, is springing up all over the world. Bible-believing Christians in Africa, in Eastern Europe, in Canada, and in Latin America are beginning to participate more in the political process. More people of faith are getting elected to public office and are placing Israel at the forefront of their concerns. Whereas in past years, Christians would put abortion, religious education, and family values as among the main issues when evaluating a candidate for office, today we're seeing *Israel* become a key issue.

As a result, wherever in the world there is a significant population of Bible-believing Christians, there's more support for Israel. In contrast, those places where the Christian population is declining due to the persecution of Christians – such as in Western Europe and Russia – there's less support for Israel. And I believe the global clash of morals, manifesting in many differing political positions, will come to a head on the issue of Israel.

In the previous chapter, we explained how, in some cases, President Trump took the values of his Bible-believing Christians support group and approached certain key situations from a Judeo-Christian viewpoint. This stance dictated practical changes in the Middle East, which brought Israel and America closer together. The two most-recognized examples are the decision to move the US embassy to Jerusalem and scrapping the Iran deal. But, if there was a top-ten list of positive moves the US could make to help Israel, Trump has already accomplished nine of them.

In addition to Jerusalem and Iran, another important decision by President Trump was to support the Taylor Force Act. Taylor Force was a young man from Lubbock, Texas, who graduated from West Point and became a veteran of the wars in Afghanistan and Iraq. After his military service, he was accepted into the Owen Graduate School of Management at Vanderbilt University. As part of a study program there, he visited Israel in 2016. While touring, he was stabbed to death in Tel Aviv by a Palestinian terrorist. After that terrorist was subsequently shot by Israeli police, Palestinians danced in the streets to celebrate their "martyr."

The murder of Taylor Force was not a random incident. The Palestinian Authority runs a widespread "pay to slay" program that pays a monthly salary – as a reward and enticement – to any imprisoned terrorist who murders civilians in Israel. This practice is fixed in the Palestinian government's laws, which describe those who attack Israel as "an integral part of the weave of Arab Palestinian society."[30] If the murderer is killed, the money is given to his family. And the more carnage, the greater the gift. Such stipends provide a big incentive for people living in a society with 20 percent unemployment and where the average monthly salary is meager.

Meanwhile, the United States was giving hundreds of millions in economic aid to the Palestinian Authority, which was then using the funds – a budget of $350 million in 2017 – to reward terrorism, including a monthly stipend to the family of the man who murdered Taylor Force. In effect, the United States taxpayers were indirectly contributing to the terrorist who murdered an American war hero.

Under the direction of President Trump, America put a stop to this terrible policy by cutting funding to the Palestinian Authority. This decision sent a strong message to the Palestinian leadership that they need to choose between financing terror and doing what's best for their people. The United States taking such a position, while morally justified, came with plenty of warnings: If you diminish the funding to the PA, people feared, the Palestinians will respond with increased attacks against Israel. It will collapse the peace process. Yet when Trump signed the Taylor Force Act into law, nothing happened.

Another significant decision by President Trump was to defund the United Nations Relief and Works Agency for Palestine Refugees in the Near East (UNRWA), the body in the UN that deals with the Palestinian refugees. All other refugees in the world are handled by a separate agency, the United Nations High Commissioner for Refugees (UNHCR), whose aim is to resettle the refugees and assist them in integrating into their new countries. But the aim of UNRWA is to perpetuate the refugee problem, not solve it.

The Palestinian refugee problem is also complicated by the ambiguous way UNRWA classifies someone as a refugee. The original group of people who later came to be known as Palestinians were Arabs who came to work in Israel during the time that the land was under British control. During the 1948 War of Independence, these Arabs left the country. Many attempted to return to their places of origin – Syria, Lebanon, and Jordan – but the authorities in those places prevented them from coming back to their villages because they wanted them to remain in the State of Israel so that they could challenge the Jewish majority there.

As a result, these families are still being held in refugee camps – seventy-two years later. Furthermore, nobody really knows the original number of displaced people because historically this region was open to traveling tribes and had no defined borders; it was not considered distinct from any other place in the Middle East. In fact, the first census taken in the Middle East was in Lebanon during the 1930s.

To add to this ambiguity in numbers (and the issue of who can claim the "right to return"), not all the current refugees are linked to the original group of Palestinians. During the 1950s, for example, the Lebanese government was unstable, and in response to internal disputes, many Lebanese citizens fled to live inside the Palestinian refugee camps, where the United Nations Relief and Works Agency offered them free food. These people from Lebanon, despite never having lived in Israel, are counted as Palestinian refugees by UNRWA.

According to the standard definition of "refugee" in the UNHCR, someone can only be considered a refugee for one generation, with the right to return for ten years. Palestinians, however, can maintain their refugee status for multiple generations. The result is that we now have five generations that are counted as Palestinian refugees, even though only around thirty thousand remain from the time of the War of Independence. According to this way of counting – a concocted classification method created specifically for this group of people – the number of refugees reaches to millions. Additionally, the agency considers any Palestinian living anywhere in the world to be a refugee. In short, UNRWA has totally different criteria than any other agency in the world for classifying someone as a refugee.

UNRWA not only maintains their status as refugees instead of resettling them but also saturates them with an anti-Israel education that promotes more division and aggression. The natural consequences of their entire operation are clearly contrary to the entire peace process. So long as this organization continues these practices, the refugees will never relocate and become normal citizens. After all, Palestinian refugees get four times the budget from the UN than do all the refugees in the world (whether the refugees are from Syria or Africa) *combined.*

Now, a critical thinker, assessing this abnormal situation, would immediately question why, when it comes to the conflict in Israel, there is a singular agency – dealing only with one group of refugees in the world – with different rules that allow the status of a refugee to transfer to descendants without any time limit. From a political and even a humanitarian perspective, that protocol makes no sense. But from a biblical perspective, this focus on one group is clear.

The motivation behind this unique treatment of refugees is not because the United Nations cares more about helping them than they do about any other group, but because perpetuating their struggle serves as a publicity weapon against Israel. Likewise, the dysfunctional system in UNRWA is not a case of well-intended attempts with unintentional harm; it is a purposeful piece of a political plan by many Muslim countries to continue criticizing Israel. After the Yom Kippur War in 1973, when Arab countries realized that they were unable defeat Israel's military, they put all their energy into going after Israel in the UN, picking on the Jewish state in any way possible.

Finally, after decades of the United States tolerating this circus in an organization that supposedly aims to assist refugees and to foster friendly relations among nations, the Trump administration decided to apply accountability. Then–Ambassador to the UN Nikki Haley confronted UNRWA and exposed the agency's different rules for Palestinians. The US had given the Palestinians $6 billion, yet UNRWA refused any suggestions for change. When the agency wouldn't make the necessary reforms to help its own people, President Trump had the courage to tell them that they would not receive any more money.

Here again, he faced tremendous pressure. For decades people had warned against cutting funding to UNRWA, claiming that it would spark retaliation, murders and riots in the streets, or attacks on Israel. They cautioned that lessened US aid would result in the Palestinians no longer having the facilities and the means to live properly. None of that happened.

In another powerful stance under Trump, the United States withdrew from the United Nations Human Rights Council due to its biased treatment of Israel and failure to address serious abuses throughout the world. For years, we saw a situation where 193 countries were anti-American and anti-Israel. Ironically, UN representatives from countries with records of horrible human rights violations, such as Iran and Venezuela, sat on this committee that continuously singled out Israel, the only free democracy in the

Middle East. The previous administrations in America yielded to the political bias and hypocrisy because people warned that pulling out of the council would be perceived as a lack of commitment to human rights and would weaken the ability to effect change. For decades, US presidents refused to ever consider withdrawing, yet President Trump did it almost immediately. Again, there was no pushback.

Another significant move that Trump initiated was to finally recognize Israel's right to the Golan Heights. Since the Six-Day War, when Israel took the region spanning 690 square miles from Syria, the Golan Heights has been termed "disputed territory." Finally, under the Trump administration, the United States acknowledged that the Golan Heights was part of Israel, which had won that land in a defensive war – a fact Israel had been pointing to all along.

Again, many people had warned that if the US ever recognized Israel's right to the Golan Heights, Arab countries would respond by attacking Israel. It's therefore better to leave it as a disputed issue – the correct political move – they argued. But the Trump administration felt it more important to acknowledge the facts and to have that land under the control of the democratic state of Israel, rather than under the control of a dangerous dictator like Assad. That too was a bold move.

President Trump also made strides on fighting the growing problem of anti-Semitism in schools and college campuses across America by signing an executive order saying that anti-Zionism is a manifestation of anti-Semitism. This law allows federal money to be withheld from educational institutions that allow discrimination, thereby helping to ensure that hate groups no longer persecute Jewish students. He also supported the anti-BDS laws that were passed in twenty-seven states.

One of the biggest moves made by the Trump administration regarding Israel was recognizing Israel's heartland – Judea and Samaria – as "disputed territory," rather than illegal. Previously, whenever Israel built homes in Judea and Samaria, it was viewed by some countries as a war crime. Politicians, including the Obama administration, even suggested these areas as the cause of the Palestinian-Israeli conflict. Again, the State Department and foreign advisors cautioned Trump that changing the status of Judea and Samaria by removing the label of "occupied territory" would lead to bloodshed and the biggest blowup of the peace process. Of course, that didn't happen either.

Another bold decision, one that largely went unnoticed, was when President Trump shut down the Palestinian Authority embassy in Washington, DC. The PA is not recognized as a state, and therefore had no right to an embassy of its own. Yet an embassy was established in Washington, DC to further push an anti-Israel agenda. People warned that shutting down that embassy would lead to another collapse of the peace process. But Trump ignored the admonitions and closed the embassy – many people don't even know it happened.

All these changes implemented by President Trump, though important and just, were discouraged for decades. Many people claimed that if the United States dared to take even one of those steps, it would cause an explosion in a tinderbox. The question is, why has there been relative calmness, given all the doomsday scenarios that people anticipated?

Herein lies an important principle: When policies are driven by what is considered politically correct – whether trying to create a Palestinian state, trying to appease the UN, or making deals with terrorist regimes – they end up in more bloodshed. But when the biblically correct path is taken, regardless of whether it's popular, the results are greater peace and stability.

Now, even if you took the Bible completely out of the picture, the approach of requiring Israel to giving away land would be suicidal for an already tiny country. While most people suggesting such a political resolution and those who oppose it have the same objective – peace – the core argument is how best to achieve it. I believe that from a cultural, military, and political perspective, the only solution that works is what former president Ronald Reagan, in his stance on Russia, called "peace through strength." Coming to a bully, a terrorist organization, or a dictatorship and promising to meet their demands if only they stop their aggression doesn't work – to avert their aggression, you must show strength.

This principle is especially true in the Middle East, where violence is the name of the game. Israel must establish a situation in which the world knows that this little country surrounded by enemies is not going to be pushed around. In Middle Eastern culture, the concept of peace between countries – *salem* – is not the same as in the Western world. The notion of peace in the eyes of most Middle Eastern leaders is a truce or ceasefire. Recognizing the culture in the region, it should be clear why all concessions by Israel had the effect of encouraging more terror.

But morality, logic, and practicality can easily become clouded in the face of political pressure. When promoting their strategies for peace in the Middle East, politicians begin with the premise that everyone wants a better life – the way it's defined in Western cultures – and therefore, there is no better plan than dividing the land. The Muslim dictators don't see it that way. They're looking at Israel through a religious lens of Islam, wherein the minute there's a powerful party in control – such as Hamas – they're going to attack Israel.

And if the enemies of Israel are looking from a biblical point of view and refusing to acknowledge the existence of a Jewish state, it only makes sense that we too look through a biblical point of view when trying to understand how to best navigate the peace process.

Similarly, the battle for Jerusalem by the Muslim world is not really about the land (Mecca and Medina are their holiest cities) but part of a wider religious war to prove the validity of Islam. The main challenge that world leaders face is whether to succumb to the false narrative about Jerusalem (which seeks to undermine the historical connection between this city and the Jewish people) and to a mindset that refuses to tolerate other religions. So long as the Arabs believe that there's a chance to gain control of Jerusalem through pushing the Palestinian story line, violence will continue. But the stronger Israel is, the more they back off and the safer the area becomes – the opposite of the way many people perceive the peace process.

Only a wiser moral compass based on fundamental biblical tenets should dictate policy. In this context, it's wrong for the United States to give terrorists money, to deny the relationship between Israel and Judea and Samaria, or to give an area critical to safety such as the Golan Heights to a violent dictator like Assad. And because President Trump acted in line with these principles, real peace and security is now closer.

This solid stance by America brought about a shift in the peace process. As long as the world bought in to the questionable status of Jerusalem and refused to move their embassies, the enemies of Israel knew their propaganda war was working. Now that Trump has made it clear that Jerusalem is off the table, that Judea and Samaria are not illegal, that the United States recognizes the Golan Heights as belonging to Israel, there is finally a real chance for peace. Moderate countries in the Middle East have begun standing alongside Israel. And therefore, if all the countries moved their embassies to Jerusalem, much of the violence and the media war would cease. The only issue left on the table is finding an alternative to the two-state solution. And if the Palestinian Authority is not willing to come to the negotiation table, then there may be a regional solution that involves some of the neighboring countries.

Despite what experts in the State Department and foreign affairs advisors have warned over the years, Trump's policies have been successful because the Bible, not some man-made peace plan governed by a political agenda, is the only sound road map for Israel. Following fundamental biblical principles – that the land belongs to the Jewish people and cannot be given away, that lives of Israeli citizens should not be endangered by funding a Palestinian leadership run by terrorists – leads to blessings, economic prosperity, and happiness for all the citizens.

Israel has blossomed and consistently ranks among the top countries on the World Happiness Report. This includes the growing Christian population and Israeli Arabs, who have the highest life expectancy among Islamic or Arab countries. Israel's standing around the world is at an all-time high. Its economy is growing at an all-time high rate. As former US ambassador to the UN Nikki Haley said, "I think we're starting to see a shift, that countries are realizing we are blessed to have Israel in the Middle East, and even the Arab countries are starting to realize that. You can't destroy what God has blessed, and Israel is blessed."[31]

While America is taking the lead by implementing policies that protect the security of Israel, the European Union is taking the exact opposite position. Though President Trump pulled out of the deal with Iran, slowing down the nuclear process, the EU is still holding to the Iran deal, even though Iran has broken it time and again. Iran is still testing ballistic missiles, selling weapons, and spending the funding it receives on terrorism. Iran is still murdering its own people, waging wars in Lebanon, Syria, and Afghanistan, and is still shouting, "Death to Israel" and "Death to America."

When it came to Jerusalem, President Trump was willing to acknowledge the facts – that Jerusalem is the capital of Israel. The administration recognized that since all other US embassies are in capitals, it was only fitting that their embassy be in Jerusalem. The EU opposed recognizing Jerusalem as the undivided capital of Israel. Instead, they've increased funding to the Palestinian Authority, even though these funds are being used to pay murderers.

While President Trump cut funding to UNRWA because of their corrupt system, the EU increased its funding to UNRWA. While more than half of US states have adopted legislation to stop BDS, the EU has accepted BDS. Furthermore, they've passed an EU regulation that all goods produced in Judea, Samaria, Jerusalem, and Golan need to be labeled, according to EU law, as made in "occupied territory" – even the Golan, where there are no Palestinians.

The same contrast in approach applies to the other changes initiated by Trump. He issued a presidential order to help prevent anti-Semitism on campuses; the EU is promoting anti-Semitism by once again labeling and singling out Jewish-made goods. Trump closed the PA embassy in Washington, DC; the EU strengthened diplomatic ties with the PA. The US officially withdrew from the UNHRC, refusing to "remain a part of a hypocritical and self-serving organization that makes a mockery of human rights."[32] The EU supports the UNHCR.

From a biblical perspective, the fact that the European Union and its policies are diametrically opposed to the US policies not only affects Israel and the Jewish people but impacts the successes of those countries. As America is supporting Israel, it has enjoyed increased success and a booming economy. Relations to other world powers are strengthening. And while Europe is supporting the PA and standing against Israel, European economies are shrinking. They're dealing with Brexit. They have enormous immigration problems.

These results echo God's promise to Abraham and his descendants: "And I will bless those who bless you, and the one who curses you I will curse…" (Genesis 12:3). And if the leaders of the EU and United States continue this trajectory, we'll likely see the downfall of Europe and further strengthening of America, as ultimately countries are judged on how they deal with God's people and the State of Israel.

CHAPTER 15

The Blessing or the Curse

It is no coincidence that Christians and Jews are finally coming together in the very same city where they parted ways more than two thousand years ago. I am often reminded of King Solomon's words: "To every thing there is a season, and a time to every purpose under heaven" (Ecclesiastes 3:1). The twenty-first century has brought a new season of change, and for anyone with faith, who has eyes to see, it is clear that we have a grand purpose under heaven – and the time to act is now.

But to determine the best course of action, it is important to first reflect on how far we have come, in a relatively short span, and where we currently stand in the big picture. Within these pages, we have taken an intense journey. We began from a period where polytheism pervaded Roman culture, when General Titus destroyed the Temple in Jerusalem and sent the Jewish people into a prolonged and stormy exile. For the next two thousand years, the Jewish people were dispersed across the world, ruthlessly persecuted for their faith. Yet they remained a people apart, preserved their sacred traditions, and never abandoned hope that they would one day reunite in their homeland.

Today, the Jewish people are finally back in Israel. Against all odds, Israel continues to flourish. Enthralled visitors and inspired immigrants pour in from around the world. Some travel there to marvel at the plethora of modern innovations; others come to breathe in the spiritual air while walking along the same ancient streets where biblical personalities rose to prominence. Just being in the land provides a religious experience. In the same vein, the Ministry of Tourism in Israel has a fantastic slogan: "If you like the book, you will love the country."

But after light comes darkness. And history repeats itself. The age-old virus of anti-Semitism has resurfaced and is spreading in the form of anti-Zionism. Israel faces daily threats of terrorism stemming from neighboring governments that espouse the teachings of radical Islam, deny Israel's right to exist, and seek Arab domination over the entire land they call Palestine. Arab broadcasts throughout the Middle East are flooded with violent animosity toward Jews. Young schoolchildren are educated about the evil intention of the Zionists and encouraged to engage in violent activity. In America, hatred takes a shrewder form. Anti-Israel bias has penetrated the liberal media and academia, where many professors feed their students an oversimplified and distorted view of the conflict, driven primarily by resentment.

Until recently, Israel – like the Jewish people throughout history – stood alone amid a hostile environment and needed to continually defend itself from libelous accusations. Now, for the first time, Israel has a global network of advocates. Bible-believing Christians in different continents are openly backing Israel, willing to swim against the current and stand up for what is right. Recognizing this surge of support coming from Christian communities led to the formation of the Knesset Christian Allies Caucus in 2004.

This caucus, consisting of a cross section of Knesset members, provides a forum for direct communication and coordination between the Knesset and Christian organizations around the world. Representatives from both groups now meet face to face to discuss the most critical issues. The popularity of the KCAC serves as a signal to the world of the close ties between these two groups based on their faith and common values. News of the caucus's accomplishments has galvanized Christian grassroots supporters of Israel, who are using faith-based diplomacy to effect positive change.

In America, Bible-believing Christians have a president who has implemented significant changes in line with their views – both by rectifying the grave mistakes of the previous administrations and by taking bold new steps. This current leadership reflects a new trend. Previously, Bible-believing Christians looked for a squeaky-clean candidate with a conservative background and wholesome family values to represent them. While campaigning, these men made all the right assurances; yet when elected to office, they were not able to follow through. Every presidential candidate since 1995, for example, pledged to move the embassy to Jerusalem; none of them did it.

The election in 2016 marked a shift wherein Bible-believing Christians opted to help elect someone who they believed had the fortitude to deliver on his promises. While Donald Trump didn't fit the profile of a Christian leader, they determined it preferable to have someone strong and able to represent their views. Trump proved to be the right choice, one of the few politicians who kept his word.

Because Bible-believing Christians in America have a leader like President Trump who is willing to listen to them, we've seen some of the most critical changes in America's relationship with

Israel, which now gives real peace a chance. The only path to peace comes from following the biblical guidelines – recognizing the Jewish people's connection to the land of Israel and ensuring the safety of its citizens – rather than taking the politically correct route at the expense of Israel's well-being. For men and women of faith, Trump's policies on Israel, driven by his Christian supporters, are part of a series of biblical prophecies.

To counteract the malign efforts of Israel's enemies, a great global awakening has occurred wherein men and women of faith are rising in their political echelons. Christians around the world will continue to support candidates willing to implement policies in line with the biblical values they treasure. Today, it is Christians, not countries, who are standing with Israel.

The wise saying "the farther backward you can look, the farther forward you can see," attributed to Winston Churchill, emphasizes the need to reflect on past events to better determine how to navigate in the future. In this context, we must take the harsh lessons of history to heart. One lesson is that Jews have functioned as the canary in the coal mine for tolerance and liberty.

In other words, the treatment of the Jews is the world's alarm system. When the ancient evil and irrational hatred of anti-Semitism is permitted to run loose and unchecked, nobody is safe – and all mankind suffers. Europeans should be familiar with this lesson. Not long ago, the alarm was sounded loudly in Europe, but few paid much attention to the vibrations. As a result, six million Jews were slaughtered. But twenty times as many non-Jewish citizens also paid with their lives.

Notwithstanding all the current freedoms, rights, and luxuries people enjoy in America, we live in a peculiar age of moral confusion. Even the finest universities teach that notions of good and evil, right and wrong, are always subjective. This secular philosophy – a departure from biblical values – is often fraught with hypocrisy and double standards in action. When it comes to the subject of Israel, for example, labels of evil imperialism and denunciation of the Zionist regime are freely tossed around in a spirit of moral superiority. At the same time, violence against innocent Israelis is advocated in the name of Palestinian liberation. Yet when it comes to denouncing murderous leaders of authoritarian regimes such as Castro, terrorist activity in Iran, or the invasiveness and repression within Sharia law, suddenly tolerance and diplomacy are emphasized.

When former president Ronald Reagan called the former Soviet Union an evil empire because of its brutal activities and suffocation of religious practices, or when former president George W. Bush used the phrase "axis of evil" to describe regimes that sponsored terrorism, much of the liberal media reacted to these statements with condescension and amusement. That same scornful attitude is now being applied to everything President Trump does, even when he takes a strong moral stance and the results prove to be fruitful.

When it comes to evaluating policies, the personality of any politician is irrelevant – action and results are primary. And two of the most telling signs of a presidential candidate's morality and competency – things that impact the world the most – are economic programs and position on Israel. The fact that after all the suffering in recent history and the success of free democracies, so many well-meaning people in America embraced a Democratic candidate like Bernie Sanders who sought to implement socialist policies and who embraced anti-Semites is a testament to how blind and forgetful people in this generation can be – another sign of the intensifying clash of civilizations.

Nevertheless, I believe that if Christians continue to strongly support President Trump, he will win a second term. But in a spiritual battle, the more important something is, the more resistance is encountered. When presented with the opportunity to do what's morally right, yet controversial, a leader always faces political pressure. With all the notable progress that Trump's policies have demonstrated, we have arrived at a crossroads.

I believe the big test will be the Deal of the Century, not the coronavirus as many people suggest. If President Trump repeats the missteps of his predecessors who mainly sought political solutions – such as "land for peace" and the two-state solution, which have failed miserably – more death, destruction, and chaos is likely to ensue. As a result, he could lose everything he worked to achieve, including the esteem of Christian supporters. But if he maintains a biblically correct vision for Israel, his policies can help create the most incredible redemption of Judea and Samaria along with the entire land of Israel – leading to a period of sustained peace and prosperity like we've never seen.

The legacy of President Trump will ultimately be judged by such decisions. Will he continue in the ways of King Cyrus the Great, who aided the Jewish people's return to their land, or will he end up compromising the security of Israel?

Moving forward, the only way to ensure this viable path to harmony and success is for those people whose vision adheres to biblical principles to get more involved in the political process – to make their voices heard – whether by voting for the best candidates, pushing their agenda, or by running for office to help defend God's covenant with Israel. The more that happens, the greater the likelihood of finding correct solutions based on biblical values. These values are the source of our strength and the reason for our country flourishing. And as faith-based diplomacy continues to bring positive change, Jews and Christians will then share in God's blessings.

Though these times are turbulent and trying, there's no reason for despair. This story – its beginning, its middle, and its end – has been foretold. As Jews and Christians continue to come together around the world, and as their representatives turn biblical support into real political action, I, along with all men and women of faith, take great comfort in knowing that there will ultimately be peace in Jerusalem. God is shining his light on the world through his people, Israel, and the best is yet to come.

Endnotes

1 The summary of the legal history of the State of Israel has been drawn from Israel Allies Foundation, "Resolution Rejecting the Misrepresentation of Israel as an Occupier and Reaffirming the Modern Jewish State's Biblical and Legal Rights to the Land of Israel and Jerusalem as Its Eternal and Indivisible Capital," signed by the participants of the 2016 Chairman's Conference and presented to the Israeli government.

2 Abigail Klein Leichman, "Top 12 New Fruit and Vegetables Developed in Israel," *Israel21c*, May 28, 2013, https://www.israel21c .org/top-12-new-fruit-and-vegetables-species-developed-in -israel/.

3 "Israeli Scientist Wins EU Innovation Award for Breath Test Device That Detects Diseases," *NoCamels Israeli Innovation News*, November 26, 2018, https://nocamels.com/2018/11/hossam -haick-technion-eu-award-sniffphone/; and see the company website at https://www.sniffphone.eu/.

4 Hillel Fendel and Chaim Silberstein, "Even Muslims Know: Jerusalem Is the Key," *Jewish Press*, February 12, 2016, https:// www.jewishpress.com/indepth/columns/keeping-jerusalem /even-muslims-know-jerusalem-is-the-key/2016/02/12/.

5 Sebastian Cahill and Audry Jeonglast, "ASUC Committee Votes 'No' on Resolution That Would Condemn Bears for Palestine,"

Daily Californian, February 12, 2020, https://www.dailycal
.org/2020/02/12/asuc-committee-votes-no-on-resolution-that
-would-condemn-bears-for-palestine/.

6   Northeastern University Students for Justice in Palestine, March
10, 2020, https://www.facebook.com/nusjp/photos/a.15063749
8428009/1537679753057103/?type=3&theater.

7   Charles Krauthammer, "Europe's Enduring Disease: Anti-
Semitism," *Chicago Tribune*, January 30, 2015, https://www
.chicagotribune.com/opinion/commentary/ct-auschwitz-israel
-jews-perspec-0130-20150129-story.html.

8   Christine Douglass-Williams, "Saudi Arabia: Christian Tourists
Will Be Arrested if They Display Bible in Public," Jihad Watch,
October 18, 2019, https://www.jihadwatch.org/2019/10/saudi
-arabia-christian-tourists-will-be-arrested-if-they-display-bible
-in-public.

9   Justus Reid Weiner, "Palestinian Crimes against Christian
Arabs and Their Manipulation against Israel," September
19, 2008, Jerusalem Center for Public Affairs, https://jcpa
.org/article/palestinian-crimes-against-christian-arabs-and
-their-manipulation-against-israel/; Raymond Ibrahim, "The
Suppressed Plight of Palestinian Christians," *Jewish Press*, June
20, 2019, https://www.jewishpress.com/indepth/opinions/the
-suppressed-plight-of-palestinian-christians/2019/06/20/.

10   Martin Sherman, "Note to Newt (Part I): Uninventing
Palestinians," *Jerusalem Post*, December 16, 2011, https://
www.jpost.com/Opinion/Columnists/Note-to-Newt-Part-I
-Uninventing-Palestinians.

11   Elhanan Miller. "About That 10,000-Year History in Jericho,
Mr. Erekat," *Times of Israel*, February 12, 2014, https://www
.timesofisrael.com/about-that-10000-year-history-in-jericho
-mr-erekat/.

12 "Accession : Estonia, Israel and Slovenia invited to join OECD," OECD, May 10,2010, https://www.oecd.org/estonia /accessionestoniaisraelandsloveniainvitedtojoinoecd.htm.

13 "The Israeli Economy Today," Consulate General of Israel to the Pacific Northwest, https://embassies.gov.il/san-francisco /AboutIsrael/Economy/Pages/The-Israeli-Economy-Today.aspx.

14 "About Intel Israel," https://www.intel.com/content/www/us/en /corporate-responsibility/intel-in-israel.html.

15 "Microsoft's Israel R&D Center," Israel Economic Mission to Canada, https://itrade.gov.il/canada/microsofts-israel-rd-center/.

16 Joseph Morgenstern, "Apple's history and development in Israel, *Jerusalem Post*, February 26, 2015, https://www.jpost.com/business /apples-history-and-development-in-israel-392387.

17 See http://israeltechgate.com/.

18 Jamie McIntyre. "Here's How Much Ground ISIS Has Lost Since Trump Took Over," *Washington Examiner*, December 23, 2017, https://www.washingtonexaminer.com/heres-how-much-ground -isis-has-lost-since-trump-took-over.

19 Steven Stalinsky, "Palestinian Authority Sermons 2000–2003," Middle East Media Research Institute, December 26, 2003, https://www.memri.org/reports/palestinian-authority-sermons -2000-2003.

20 Sheikh Abdul Hadi Palazzi, "Allah Is a Zionist," *Tablet*, https:// www.tabletmag.com/jewish-news-and-politics/28575/allah-is -a-zionist.

21 David DesRoches, "Connecticut College Professor Accused of Racist, Anti-Palestinian Facebook Post," National Public Radio, March 25, 2015, https://www.wnpr.org/post/connecticut-college -professor-accused-racist-anti-palestinian-facebook-post.

22   Max Kutner, "Matisyahu Dropped from Concert Lineup for Not Endorsing Palestine," *Newsweek*, August 16, 2015, https://www .newsweek.com/matisyahu-concert-canceled-palestine-363350.

23   Lindy Lowry, "In Africa, Christians Are in the Flames of Persecution—and on Fire for Jesus," Open Doors, May 21, 2019, https://www.opendoorsusa.org/christian-persecution/stories/in -africa-christians-are-in-the-flames-of-persecution-and-on-fire -for-jesus/.

24   Kate Shellnutt, "Terrorists in Burkina Faso Execute Six at Pentecostal Church," *Christianity Today*, April 30, 2019, https://www .christianitytoday.com/news/2019/april/burkina-faso-assemblies -god-church-attack-six-dead-pastor.html; Lee Brown, "Burkina Faso Church Attack Leaves 5 Dead, Including Priest," *New York Post*, April 29, 2019, https://nypost.com/2019/04/29 /burkina-faso-church-attack-leaves-five-dead-including-priest/.

25   Justus Reid Weiner, "Palestinian Crimes against Christian Arabs and Their Manipulation against Israel," Jerusalem Center for Public Affairs, September 19, 2008, https://jcpa.org/article/palestinian -crimes-against-christian-arabs-and-their-manipulation-against -israel/.

26   Linda Sarsour (@lsarsour), Twitter, May 13, 2015, 6:21 a.m., https:// twitter.com/lsarsour/status/598327052727615488?lang=en.

27   "Women's Rights in Iran," Human Rights Watch, October 28, 2015, https://www.hrw.org/news/2015/10/28/womens-rights-iran.

28   Jessica Chasmar, "Colin Kaepernick Slams American Terrorist Attacks against Black and Brown People after Iran Strike," *Washington Times*, January 6, 2020, https://www.washingtontimes.com /news/2020/jan/6/colin-kaepernick-slams-american-terrorist -attacks-/.

29 Caroline Glick, "Donald Trump and the Mythmakers," *Jewish World Review*, January 13, 2020, http://www.jewishworldreview.com /0120/glick011320.php3.

30 Michael Barbero, Sander Gerber, and Michael Makovsky, "Congress Is Overdue to Pass the Taylor Force Act," *The Hill*, March 4, 2018, https://thehill.com/opinion/national-security /376663-congress-is-overdue-to-pass-the-taylor-force-act.

31 "Nikki Haley: 'The Better and Stronger We Make Israel, the Safer We Make the World,'" Jewish News Syndicate, June 28, 2019, https://www.jns.org/nikki-haley-the-better-and-stronger-we -make-israel-the-safer-we-make-the-world/.

32 "U.S. Announces Its Withdrawal from U.N. Human Rights Council," National Public Radio, June 19, 2018, https://www .npr.org/2018/06/19/621435225/u-s-announces-its-withdrawal -from-u-n-s-human-rights-council.

About the Author

Josh Reinstein has been the director of the Knesset Christian Allies Caucus since its inception on January 5, 2004, and is also president of the Israel Allies Foundation. He is the producer and founder of the hit TV show *Israel Now News*, a half-hour weekly news magazine broadcast to millions of viewers around the world. He also owns and operates JSR International Marketing, an international marketing and investment firm based in Israel.

Josh Reinstein grew up in Dallas, Texas and Toronto, Canada. He is a graduate of the University of Western Ontario, where he earned a degree in political science. He served as a tank gunner in the elite 188 unit of the Israel Defense Forces Armored Corps. He currently lives in a suburb of Jerusalem with his wife Rebekah and their four children.

Mr. Reinstein was named one of the "50 Most Influential Jews" by the *Jerusalem Post*.